# Essential
# Ireland

**AAA Publishing** 1000 AAA Drive, Heathrow, Florida 32746

**Ireland:** Regions and Best places to see

**Original text by Penny Phenix**
Revised and updated by Chris Bagshaw

Edited, designed and produced by AA Publishing
© AA Media Limited 2011

978-1-59508-417-0

Published in the United States by AAA Publishing,
1000 AAA Drive, Heathrow, Florida 32746
Published in the United Kingdom by AA Publishing

Color separation: AA Digital Department
Printed and bound in Italy by Printer Trento S.r.l.

A04193

Republic of Ireland mapping based on Ordnance Survey Ireland.
Permit number 8634. © Ordnance Survey Ireland and Government
of Ireland.
Maps based upon Crown Copyright and is reproduced with the
permission of Land & Property Services under delegated authority
from the Controller of Her Majesty's Stationery Office, © Crown
copyright and database rights 2011. Licence no. 100062.
Permit no. 100062

# About this book

This book is divided into five sections.

**The essence of Ireland** pages 6–19
Introduction; Features; Food and drink; Short break

**Planning** pages 20–33
Before you go; Getting there; Getting around; Being there

**Best places to see** pages 34–55
The unmissable highlights of any visit to Ireland

**Best things to do** pages 56–77
Good places to have lunch; stunning scenery; top activities; boat trips; places to take the children; traditional music and more

**Exploring** pages 78–186
The best places to visit in Ireland, organized by area

**Maps** All map references are to the maps on the covers. For example, Cork has the reference ✚ 18L – indicating the grid square in which it can be found.

**Admission prices**
Inexpensive (under €5/£3.75);
Moderate (€5–€10/£3.75–£7.50);
Expensive (over €10/£7.50)

**Hotel prices** Room per night.
Republic of Ireland/Northern Ireland:
**€/£** budget (under €100/£75);
**€€/££** moderate (€100–€175/£75–£130);
**€€€/£££** expensive (over €175/£130)

**Restaurant prices** A three-course meal per person without drinks.
Republic of Ireland/Northern Ireland:
**€/£** budget (under €25/£19);
**€€/££** moderate (€25–€50/£19–£37);
**€€€/£££** expensive (over €50/£37)

# Contents

# The essence of...

Ask visitors what attracted them to Ireland and the chances are they will rave about green hills, Guinness-filled pubs and friendly locals always ready for a chat – or a song. Ireland does have all this, but also so much more – from superb landscapes to ancient sites and stately homes – that if your time is limited you will need to be selective.

Ireland has great cities in each of its four quarters – Dublin in the east, Belfast in the north, Limerick and Galway in the west and Cork in the south – and just a short visit to each will demonstrate the differences in character between these regions.

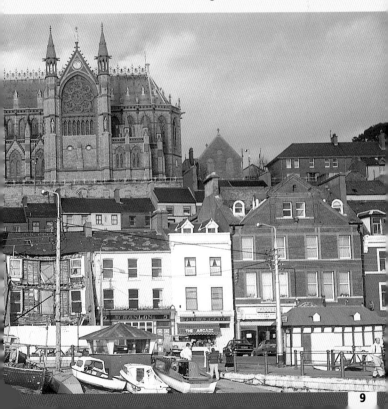

features

Back in the 1980s, though the scenery was magical and the hospitality wonderful, there was undercurrent of sadness in Ireland at the ailing economy and the rampant depopulation, particularly among the young. Many properties were being snapped up by outsiders for holiday homes, which would stand empty for much of the year.

Visiting the Republic today you will find that the magic in the scenery and the welcoming people remain unchanged. But in the 1990s, with a generous taxation system and funding from the EU, Ireland's economy took off in dramatic style. Migrants returned, graduates stayed and new building sprang up all over Ireland. These "Celtic Tiger" years ended with the recession of the late 2000s, but the legacy is everywhere. Motorways, hotels, public transport and some major foreign

investors remain in a land that has fundamentally changed. But this is still Ireland. As of old, nothing is so urgent that it should stand in the way of a good conversation with someone you have only just met. Do not be deterred from visiting Northern Ireland, where the political violence has ended and you'll be impressed with the friendliness of the locals, the beautiful scenery, the interesting historic buildings and the many cultural activities.

## GEOGRAPHY

● Ireland lies on the continental shelf to the west of the European mainland. To the east, over the Irish Sea, lies Britain, with Scotland 21km (13 miles) to the northeast.

● In area, Ireland is 7 million hectares (17.3 million acres) and of those, around a third are devoted to agriculture.

● Cork is the largest county and Louth the smallest.

● The highest mountain is Carrantuohill, 1,041m (3,415ft), in the Macgillycuddy's Reeks range of Co Kerry.

● The longest river is the Shannon at 340km (210 miles), while the largest lake is Lough Neagh at 396sq km (153sq miles).

● Ireland has some of Europe's emptiest and cleanest beaches, with great expanses of silvery sands and little rocky coves.

● There are thousands of lakes in Ireland, particularly in the "lakeland counties", which extend southwards from the border with Northern Ireland, and in Connemara.

● Ireland has a large number of nature reserves that are rich in animal and plant life, and the national parks preserve some large areas of great beauty.

## SPORT AND LEISURE

● Salmon season: January to September.

● Brown trout season: 15 February to 12 October.

● Sea trout fishing: June to September (or 12 October in some places).

● There is no close season for coarse fishing, and sea angling is possible all year round.

● Ireland has over 11,000 pubs.

● There are more than 400 golf courses in Ireland.

● Horse racing is very popular, with the Grand National in April and the Irish Derby in June.

food & drink

**Eating out in Ireland is as unhurried an experience as anything else in this relaxing island, and the generally high standard of cooking and service, and the quality of the ingredients, are certainly well worth savouring.**

In all the major towns and cities there is a good variety of food on offer, and traditional Irish cuisine has enjoyed a revival, often with the occasional international influence. Away from the fast-food places, eating out in Ireland is not particularly cheap, but travellers on a budget will find a choice of restaurants throughout the country which offer a "tourist menu" of good food at reasonable prices.

Specialities to look for include local cheeses, of which there are many, such as the delicious Cashel Blue, Cooleeney, St Killian, Durrus, Chetwynd Blue

and Mizen. Irish seafood is also legendary, with fresh lobster, oysters, mussels and scallops.

## IRISH CUISINE

Irish cooking has a reputation for being plain but plentiful, which does it something of a disservice, because the traditional dishes have wonderfully rich flavours and interesting taste combinations.

In recent years dishes that were designed to satisfy the hunger of hard-working farmers and fishermen have been adapted to suit the lesser appetites of those who have done no more than a bit of gentle sightseeing. What was once dismissed as "peasant food" has now become a delicacy, such as *drisheen* (black pudding), *cruibeens* (pigs' trotters), Dublin coddle (a sausage stew), beef stewed in Guinness and, of course, Irish stew.

Potato dishes such as *champ* (mashed with chives and butter) or *colcannon* (mashed, mixed with leek, butter, cabbage, cream and nutmeg) are a tasty accompaniment, and adventurous diners can sample edible seaweed in the form of dulce or carrageen pudding.

Irish bread is not just something to make a sandwich with. There are lots of tasty varieties that only need a spreading of butter or a side dish of home-made soup. Soda bread, or wheaten bread,

made with stone-ground flour, has a wonderful flavour and texture, and there are lots of fruity tea breads such as barm brack. There is even a potato bread (mashed potato mixed with flour and egg) that is cooked on a griddle and often served with the enormous traditional Irish breakfast of bacon, eggs, sausage and black (or white) pudding.

## WHISKEY AND BEER

Think of Irish beer and it is probably a pint of Guinness that springs to mind. Sold in at least 150 countries world-wide, Guinness is a great symbol of Irishness, but undoubtedly tastes best on Irish soil, with its cool, biting flavour

and thick creamy head. Hard on the heels of Guinness are two other stouts, Beamish and Murphy's, both brewed in Cork, while Smithwicks offers a smooth-tasting ale similar to English beer. Lager and Irish cider are both widely available.

Irish whiskey also has a world market and has a wonderful clean flavour, quite different from Scotch whisky or American bourbon. Three main brands are produced by the Irish Distillers company – Jameson, Powers and Paddy, with pure malts of various ages, as well as blended whiskey. The Bushmills Distillery in Northern Ireland (now owned by Guinness parent Diageo) and the Jameson Heritage Centre at Midleton, Co Cork give guided tours explaining the distilling process.

**short break**

If you have only a short time to visit Ireland and would like to take home some unforgettable memories, you can do something local and capture the real flavour of the country. The following suggestions will give you a wide range of sights and experiences that won't take very long, won't cost very much and will make your visit very special.

● **Drive the Ring of Kerry** (➤ 122) to see some of Ireland's most spectacular coastal and inland scenery, including huge fiord-like bays, the country's highest mountain, sparkling lakes, pretty villages and colourful hedgerows and gardens, which flourish in an exceptionally mild climate.

● **Join in a *ceilidh*** (pronounced "kaylee"), with traditional music and dancing. Lose your inhibitions and get lost in the atmosphere – you can always sing along. There are music sessions in the cities and large towns on most nights. In the country there is usually a session within easy reach,

especially in the west and in summer. Wherever you go the standard is generally very high.

- **Wander along Grafton Street** in Dublin, for the shops and the buskers (street musicians), and have a coffee at Bewley's Oriental Café. The variety of open-air acts is enormous, from penny-whistle players to classical string quartets. Check out the small streets off to the side; there are some good pubs to be found.

- **Go to a race meeting at The Curragh.** The Irish have a unique affinity with horses, and a day at the races here is quite an experience. Visit the National Stud at Kildare (➤ 95) and see the stallions in their stalls and paddocks and learn more at the Horse Museum.

- **Visit Glendalough** to soak up the atmosphere of this historic ruined monastic city (➤ 92–93) in a beautiful valley of the Wicklow Mountains. Only a short drive from Dublin, this is a world apart.

- **Look out from the Cliffs of Moher,** with no other landfall between here and North America, and contemplate the feelings of the millions of emigrants who left this beautiful country for an unknown destiny in the New World (➤ 144).

- **Visit Skibbereen on the day of the cattle market** to sample the real working life of an agricultural community, but do not be in a hurry on the road because you will be following all manner of vehicles

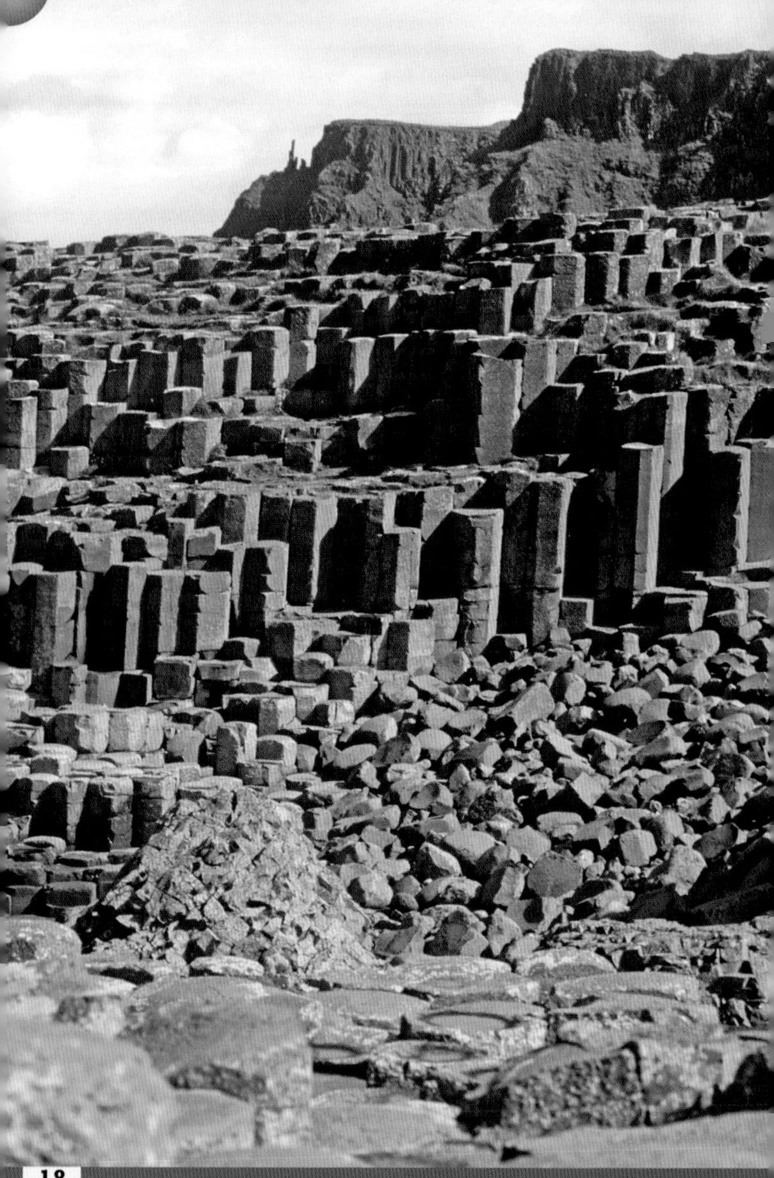

bringing livestock into town – all part of the experience.

● **For a taste of Ireland, eat oysters and drink Guinness** at Paddy Burke's Oyster Inn in Clarenbridge, Co Galway, famous for its oyster festival. To experience the oyster festival, visit Clarenbridge in September.

● **Rent a cruiser and explore the lovely River Shannon,** its lakes and the historic sites, riverside towns and villages along the way (► 64). Since the reopening of the Ballyconnell and Ballinamore Canal as the Shannon–Erne waterway in 1994 it is possible to travel from Belleek in the north through the heart of Ireland to Limerick and the Shannon Estuary.

● **Take a walk along the clifftops of Co Antrim to the Giant's Causeway** to see how ancient travellers would first have witnessed this most remarkable place (► 42–43). Drive along this coast for views of cliffs, bluffs, headlands and sandy beaches.

# Planning

# Before you go

## WHEN TO GO

| | JAN | FEB | MAR | APR | MAY | JUN | JUL | AUG | SEP | OCT | NOV | DEC |
|---|---|---|---|---|---|---|---|---|---|---|---|---|
| | 8°C | 8°C | 10°C | 13°C | 15°C | 18°C | 20°C | 19°C | 17°C | 14°C | 10°C | 8°C |
| | 46°F | 46°F | 50°F | 55°F | 59°F | 64°F | 68°F | 66°F | 63°F | 57°F | 50°F | 46°F |

High season    Low season

Temperatures are the **average daily maximum** for each month. The best weather is in spring and early summer (April and June). Winter (November to March) can be dark, wet and dreary, especially in the mountainous west, but good-weather days can be magical. In high summer (July and August) the weather is changeable and often cloudy. Autumn (September and October) generally sees good weather. The cities are great places to visit at any time, regardless of the weather, and Christmas and the New Year are particularly popular.

It will almost certainly rain at some time during your stay, no matter when you visit. Be prepared, but try to accept the rain as the Irish do, as a "wet blessing".

## WHAT YOU NEED

| | | UK | Germany | USA | Netherlands | Spain |
|---|---|---|---|---|---|---|
| ● Required  ○ Suggested  ▲ Not required | Some countries require a passport to remain valid for a minimum period (usually at least six months) beyond the date of entry – contact their consulate or embassy or your travel agent for details. | | | | | |
| Passport (or National Identity Card where applicable) | | ▲ | ● | ● | ● | ● |
| Visa (regulations can change – check before you travel) | | ▲ | ▲ | ▲ | ▲ | ▲ |
| Onward or Return Ticket | | ○ | ○ | ○ | ○ | ○ |
| Health Inoculations | | ▲ | ▲ | ▲ | ▲ | ▲ |
| Health Documentation (►23, Health Insurance) | | ● | ● | ● | ● | ● |
| Travel Insurance | | ○ | ○ | ○ | ○ | ○ |
| Driving Licence (national) | | ● | ● | ● | ● | ● |
| Car Insurance Certificate | | ● | ● | ● | ● | ● |
| Car Registration Document | | ● | ● | ● | ● | ● |

## WEBSITES
### Republic of Ireland
www.discoverireland.com
www.discoverireland.ie
www.failteireland.ie
www.shannondev.ie

www.visitdublin.com
www.dublin.ie

### Northern Ireland
www.discovernorthernireland.com

## TOURIST OFFICES AT HOME
### In the UK
Tourism Ireland (for Republic and
Northern Ireland)
103 Wigmore Street,
London W1U 1QS
☎ 0207 513 0880;
www.discoverireland.com/gb

### In the USA
Tourism Ireland (for Republic and
Northern Ireland)
345 Park Avenue,
New York, NY 10154
☎ 212/418-0800;
www.discoverireland.com/us

## HEALTH INSURANCE
**Insurance** Nationals of EU and certain other countries can get discounted
medical treatment in Ireland with a European Health Insurance Card (not
required for UK nationals), although private medical insurance is still
advised and is essential for all other visitors.

**Dental services** EU nationals or nationals of countries with which
Ireland has a reciprocal agreement can get discounted dental treatment
within the Irish health service with a European Health Insurance Card
(not needed for UK nationals). Others should take out private medical
insurance.

## TIME DIFFERENCES

| GMT | Ireland | Germany | USA (NY) | Netherlands | Spain |
|-----|---------|---------|----------|-------------|-------|
| 12 noon | 12 noon | 1PM | 7AM | 1PM | 1PM |

Ireland observes Greenwich Mean Time (GMT), but from late March,
when clocks are put forward one hour, until late October, summertime
(GMT+1) operates.

## NATIONAL HOLIDAYS

1 Jan New Year's Day
17 Mar St Patrick's Day
Mar/Apr Good Friday,
  Easter Monday
May (1st Mon)
  May Holiday
May (last Mon)
  Spring Holiday (NI)

Jun (1st Mon)
  June Holiday (RI)
12 Jul Orangeman's Day
  (NI)
Aug (1st Mon)
  August Holiday (RI)
Aug (last Mon)
  Late Summer Holiday (NI)

Oct (last Mon)
  October Holiday (RI)
25 Dec Christmas Day
26 Dec Boxing Day/
  St Stephen's Day

## WHAT'S ON WHEN

**February** *Folk Festival:* Gleneagle Hotel, Killarney, Co Kerry.
**March** *Dublin Film Festival.*
*St Patrick's Day:* various parades and pilgrimages commemorating Ireland's patron saint.
**April** *Irish Grand National:* Fairyhouse Racecourse, Co Meath.
*World Irish Dancing Championship:* the best shows, entertainments and parades at various locations.
*Antiques and Collectables Fair:* Dublin.
**May** *Fleadh Nua:* Ennis, Co Clare.
*Belfast City Carnival:* Belfast.
*Balitmore Seafood and Wooden Boat Festival:* Baltimore, Co Cork.
*Slieve Bloom Walking Festival:* Kinnitty, Co Offaly.
*The Balmoral Show:* Balmoral, Belfast.
*The Cathedral Quarter Arts Festival:* Belfast.
**June** *Limavady Jazz and Blues Festival:* Limavady, Co Londonderry.
*Bloomsday (16 June):* in honour of James Joyce's *Ulysses.*
**July** *Festival of the Erne:* Belturbet, Co Cavan.
*Galway Arts Festival:* films, music, books and plays.
*Boyle Arts Festival:* Boyle, Co Roscommon.
*Historic Sham Fight:* Scarva, Co Down.
*Independence Day Celebrations:* Ulster American Folk Park, Co Tyrone.
**August** *Ballyshannon International Folk Festival:* Ballyshannon, Co Donegal.
*Rose of Tralee Festival:* Tralee, Co Kerry.

*Fleadh Cheoil na hÉiereann (All Ireland Music Festival):* various locations.
*Puck Fair:* Killorglin, Co Kerry.
*Killarney Summerfest:* Co Kerry.
*Kinsale Regatta and Homecoming Festival:* Co Cork brings expatriates home: sailing, walking and plenty of seafood.
**September** *All Ireland Football and Hurling Finals:* Croke Park, Dublin.
*Clarenbridge Oyster Festival:* Clarenbridge, Co Galway.

*Galway International Oyster Festival:* Co Galway.
*Blackstairs Blues Festival:* Enniscorthy, Co Wexford.
*Story Telling Festival:* Cape Clear, Co Cork.
*Listowel Races:* Listowel, Co Kerry.
*Appalachian and Blue Grass Festival:* Ulster American Folk Park, Co Tyrone.
*Proms in the Park:* Hillsborough Castle, Co Down
**October** *Dublin Theatre Festival and Fringe Festival:* the best of Irish and international drama.
*Cork Jazz Festival.*
*Cork Film Festival.*
*Kinsale Gourmet Festival:* Co Cork.
*Wexford Opera Festival:* Wexford, Co Wexford.
*Belfast Festival:* at Queen's.

**November** *Foyle Film Festival:* Londonderry, Co Londonderry.
*Listowel Food Fair:* Listowel, Co Kerry.
*Waterford International Festival of Light Opera:* Waterford, Co Waterford.
*Spirit of the Voice Festival:* Galway City.
**December** *Cinemagic Film Festival:* Belfast.
*Dingle Wren:* Co Kerry. Lots of dressing up and playing tricks on 26 December.

# Getting there

## BY AIR

**Dublin Airport**

11km (7 miles) to city centre

🚃 N/A
🚌 30 minutes
🚕 20 minutes

**Belfast International Airport**

31km (19 miles) to city centre

🚃 60 minutes
🚌 45 minutes
🚕 45 minutes

**Shannon Airport**

26km (16 miles) to Limerick city centre

🚃 N/A
🚌 25 minutes
🚕 25 minutes

Scheduled flights operate from Britain, mainland Europe and North America to Dublin, Cork, Knock, Shannon and Belfast. The Republic's national airline is Aer Lingus (tel: 0818 365 0000; www.aerlingus.com).

**Dublin Airport:** By car, take the M1 south to the city centre. An Airlink bus leaves from the airport every 10 minutes, less frequently after 8pm (moderate fare, under 16s free) to the city centre via the central bus station (Busáras) and Connolly and Heuston railway stations. Taxis wait at the Arrivals area (expensive).

**Belfast International Airport:** The journey to central Belfast takes about 30 to 60 minutes. By car, follow the M2 motorway east. An Airbus 300 service (moderate fare, children free) runs every 10 minutes (sometimes hourly on Sundays). Taxi fares are expensive.

**Shannon Airport:** To get to Limerick from Shannon Airport by car, take the N18 east. Bus Éireann runs a frequent, inexpensive airport-to-Limerick/ Ennis service. Taxis are moderate to expensive.

## BY SEA

Most arrivals by sea come through Dublin Port or Dun Laoghaire, south of Dublin; Rosslare, Co Wexford, has ferry links with the UK and France.

From Dun Laoghaire port by car to Dublin, simply follow signs for the city centre. There is a frequent Dublin Bus service to Dublin city centre. Taxi fares range from moderate to expensive. An inexpensive DART service (► below) from Dun Laoghaire to Dublin runs every half-hour (often more frequently).

Belfast Ferryport: the journey to Belfast takes 10 to 15 minutes, depending on traffic. Taxi fares to Belfast city centre are moderate.

Larne Ferryport: the journey to central Belfast takes 30 to 60 minutes.

# Getting around

## PUBLIC TRANSPORT

**Internal flights** Flights from Dublin to other airports in Ireland are operated by Aer Lingus (tel: 0818 365 0000), Ryanair (tel: 0818 303030) and Aer Arann (tel: 0818 210210).

**Trains** In the Republic a limited network run by Iarnród Éireann (tel: 1850 366222) serves major towns and cities. Trains are comfortable, generally reliable and fares reasonable. Northern Ireland Railways (tel: 028 9066 6630) operates services from Belfast to main towns and to Dublin.

A light rail overground system, the Dublin Area Rapid Transit (DART), has 30 stations from Howth and Malahide in the north to Greystones in the south (www.irishrail.ie). Trains run every 5 minutes in rush hour, otherwise every 10 to 15 minutes. Tickets are available singly from any DART station, but it is more economical to buy them en bloc from Dublin Bus (59 Upper O'Connell Street), from some newsstands or at the stations. The Luas tram system has two unconnected lines linking central Dublin with the western and southern suburbs.

**Long-distance buses** In the Republic, Bus Éireann (tel: 01-836 6111) operates a network of express bus routes serving most of the country (some run summer only). In Northern Ireland, Ulsterbus (tel: 028 9066 6630) has links between Belfast and most villages and towns. Unlimited travel tickets are available.

**Urban buses** City bus services, particularly in Dublin and Belfast, are excellent. Dublin is served by Dublin Bus (tel: 01 873 4222) and the Luas, a tram system mainly serving the Dublin surburbs (www.luas.ie). Citybus (tel: 028 9066 6630) serves the Belfast area.

**Ferries** Car ferries operate between Ballyhack, Co Wexford and Passage East, Co Waterford (tel: 051 382480) and Killimer, Co Clare and Tarbert, Co Kerry (tel: 065 905 3124), the latter saving 100km (62 miles) on the road journey. There are also ferry services from the mainland to some islands.

## TAXIS

Taxis are available in major towns and cities, at taxi stands or outside hotels, and at main rail stations, ports and airports. In Belfast, black cabs may be shared by customers and some operate rather like buses, shuttling their passengers between the city and the suburbs.

You can hail or stop a taxi in Dublin in the street, or you can call them by telephone (look in the *Golden Pages*). The taxis are all metered.

## FARES AND CONCESSIONS

Students and senior citizens may be entitled to reduced entrance at some museums and galleries. Be sure to carry some form of identification. Dublin Pass (available from Dublin Tourist Office) gives generous discounts or free admission to attractions in Dublin (www.dublinpass.ie).

Many car rental companies give discounts to those over 50 or 55, as do some hotels and a few tourist attractions. Some tour companies offer special spring and autumn package deals.

## DRIVING

- Drive on the left.
- Speed limits on motorways (blue): 120kph/75mph (70mph/112kph in Northern Ireland).
- Speed limits on national roads (green): 100kph/62mph (60mph/96kph in Northern Ireland).
- Speed limits on regional and local roads (white): 80kph/50mph (Republic of Ireland only).
- Speed limits on urban roads: 50kph/30mph (or as signposted) in the Republic and Northern Ireland.
- Seat belts must be worn in front seats at all times and in rear seats where fitted.
- Random breath-testing takes place. Never drink and drive.
- Lead replacement petrol (LRP) and unleaded petrol are widely available on both sides of the border. Fuel stations in villages in the Republic stay open until 8 or 9pm, and open after Mass on Sundays. In Northern Ireland, 24-hour petrol stations are fairly common. Fuel is cheaper in Northern Ireland than in the Republic.
- If you break down driving your own car and are a member of an AIT-affiliated motoring club, you can call the Automobile Association's rescue service (tel: 1800 667788 in the Republic; tel: 0800 887766 in Northern Ireland). If the car is rented, follow the instructions given in the documentation; most of the international rental firms provide a rescue service.

## CAR RENTAL

All of the international car rental firms are represented. A car from a local company, however, is likely to offer cheaper rates, but may not allow different pick-up/drop-off points.

# Being there

## TOURIST OFFICES
- www.discoverireland.ie

## REPUBLIC OF IRELAND
- Dublin Tourism,
  Suffolk Street, Dublin 2
  www.dublin.com
- Southeast Tourism,
  41 The Quay, Waterford
  ☎ 051 875823
- Cork-Kerry Tourism,
  Grand Parade, Cork City
  ☎ 021 425 5100
- Shannon Development,
  Tourism Division,
  Shannon Town Centre,
  Co Clare
  ☎ 061 361555
- Ireland West Tourism,
  Forster Street, Galway City
  ☎ 091 537700
- Northwest Tourism,
  Temple Street, Sligo
  ☎ 071 916 1201
- East Coast & Midlands Tourism,
  Clonard House, Dublin Road,
  Mullingar, Co Westmeath ☎ 044
  934 8761

## NORTHERN IRELAND
- Tourist Information Centre,
  St Anne's Court, 59 North Street,
  Belfast BT1 1NB
  ☎ 028 9023 1221;
  www.discovernorthernireland.
  com

## MONEY
The monetary units are (in the Republic) the euro (€), and (in Northern Ireland) the pound sterling (£). These are not interchangeable. Euro notes come in denominations of €5, €10, €20, €50, €100, €200 and €500; coins in denominations of 1, 2, 5, 10, 20 and 50 cents and €1 and €2.

Pound sterling notes for Northern Ireland are in denominations of £5, £10, £20 and £50; coins are available in denominations of £1 and £2, and 1, 2, 5, 10, 20 and 50 pence.

Provincial banks also issue notes in denominations of £5, £10, £20 and £50, but these are not accepted in other parts of the UK.

## POSTAL AND INTERNET SERVICES
The main post offices in O'Connell Street, Dublin, and Castle Place, Belfast, are open extended hours, otherwise hours are 9–5:30 (Sat: 9–1 in

## TIPS/GRATUITIES

| Yes ✓ No ✕ | | |
|---|---|---|
| Restaurants/cafés (if service not included) | ✓ | 10% |
| Taxis | ✓ | 10% |
| Tour guides | ✓ | £1/€2 |
| Porters | ✓ | 50p/€1 |
| Toilets | ✕ | |

the Republic, 9–12:30 in Northern Ireland) tel: 01-705 7000 (ROI); tel: 028 9032 3740 (NI).

There are plenty of internet cafés in major urban areas and the vast majority of hotels have wireless internet access of some type, although it may not be free. Some cafés in the cities have WiFi access, usually at a small cost. Another option is to try the local public library or tourist information centre.

## TELEPHONES

Public telephone boxes, blue and grey in the Republic and red in Northern Ireland, have been largely replaced by glass and metal booths. To make a call, lift the handset, insert the correct coins (RI: 10, 20 or 50 cents, or €1, €2; NI: 10, 20 or 50 pence, or £1) or phonecard and dial.

### Emergency telephone numbers
Police, Fire, Ambulance and Coastal rescue: 999 or 112

### International dialling codes
From Ireland to:
UK: 00 44
(RI only; no code needed from NI)
Germany: 00 49
USA: 00 1
Netherlands: 00 31
Spain: 00 34

## EMBASSIES AND CONSULATES
UK ☎ 01 205 3700
Germany ☎ 028 9269 8356 (NI),
01-269 3011 (RI)
USA ☎ 028 9038 6100 (NI),
01 668 8777 (RI)

Netherlands ☎ 028 9077 9088
(NI), 01 269 3444 (RI)
Spain ☎ 0161 236 1233 (NI),
01 269 1640 (RI)

## HEALTH ADVICE

**Sun advice** May and June are the sunniest months, though July and August are the hottest. Take the normal precautions against the sun.

**Drugs** Prescription and non-prescription drugs are available from pharmacies. In an emergency, contact the nearest hospital.

**Safe water** Tap water is safe to drink. Bottled water is widely available.

## PERSONAL SAFETY

The national police forces are: RI – Garda Síochána (pronounced "sheekawnah") in black-and-blue uniforms

NI – Police Service of Northern Ireland in dark green uniforms.

● While some sectarian tensions remain in areas like some suburbs of Belfast and southern Co Armagh, there is no longer any serious violence and visitors should have no worries.

● Take care of personal property in Dublin and avoid leaving property visible in cars.

## ELECTRICITY

The power supply is: 220 volts (RI); 240 volts (NI). Sockets are three square-pin (UK type). Overseas visitors will need a travel adaptor .

## OPENING HOURS

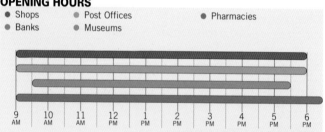

In addition to the times shown above, some shops stay open till 8 or 9pm on Thursdays and Fridays. Smaller towns and rural areas have an early closing day on one day a week. Nearly all banks close on Saturday and many post offices close at 1pm. Museums and tourist sites vary; check with a local tourist office. Many smaller places close from October to March or have very limited opening.

## LANGUAGE

The Republic has two official languages, English and Irish. Everyone speaks English, though you are likely to hear Irish spoken in the Gaeltacht areas of the west and south (Kerry, Galway, Mayo, the Aran Islands, Donegal and Waterford), where you may find road signs in Irish only. Below is a list of some words that you may come across while you are in Ireland. The official language of Northern Ireland is English.

| | | | |
|---|---|---|---|
| yes | *tá/sea* | excuse me | *gabh mo leithscéal* |
| no | *níl/ní hea* | how much? | *cé mhéid?* |
| please | *le do thoil* | open | *oscailte* |
| thank you | *go raibh maith agat* | closed | *dúnta* |
| welcome | *fáilte* | police | *gardaí* |
| hello | *dia dhuit* | toilet | *leithreas* |
| goodbye | *slán* | men | *fir* |
| goodnight | *oíche mhaith* | women | *mná* |

| | | | |
|---|---|---|---|
| hotel | *óstán* | one person | *aon duine* |
| bed and breakfast | *loístín oíche* | one night | *oíche amháin* |
| single room | *seomra singil* | chambermaid | *cailín aimsire* |
| double room | *seomra dúbailte* | room service | *seirbhís seomraí* |

| | | | |
|---|---|---|---|
| bank | *an banc* | banknote | *nóta bainc* |
| exchange office | *oifig malairte* | cheque | *seic* |
| post office | *oifig an phoist* | travellers' cheque | *seic taistil* |
| coin | *bonn* | credit card | *cárta creidmheasa* |

| | | | |
|---|---|---|---|
| restaurant | *bialann* | lunch | *lón* |
| café | *caife* | dinner | *dinnéar* |
| pub/bar | *tábhairne* | table | *tábla* |
| breakfast | *bricfeásta* | waiter | *freastalaí* |

| | | | |
|---|---|---|---|
| aeroplane | *eitleán* | station | *stáisiún* |
| airport | *aerfort* | boat | *bád* |
| train | *traein* | port | *port* |
| bus | *bus* | ticket | *ticéad* |

# Best places to see

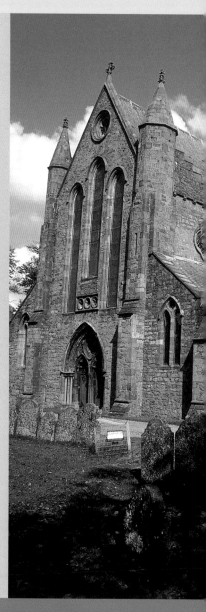

# 1 Brú na Bóinne

**The valley of the River Boyne east of Slane is a remarkable area containing evidence of Ireland's most ancient history.**

This great neolithic cemetery consists of at least 40 burial sites, and the landscape is dotted with standing stones and earthworks, but the crowning glory is the great passage grave at **Newgrange.** Older than Stonehenge, it is a mound of enormous dimensions, 11m (36ft) high and 90m (295ft) across, with a white quartzite retaining wall encircled with large kerbstones (curbstones) at its base, incised with geometric patterns. Beyond this are the 12 surviving stones of a great circle that once stretched all the way around the mound.

The entrance to the tomb is marked by a massive stone with triple spiral ornamentations, and above it is an opening through which the rays of the rising sun illuminate the interior of the central chamber for about 15 minutes on just one day of the year – the winter solstice, 21 December (the phenomenon is recreated with artificial light the rest of the year, at the end of the guided tour).

Inside the chamber it is possible to see the intricate construction of the roof, which still keeps

out water after about 5,000 years, and the recesses into which the remains of the cremated dead were placed, together with final offerings. There are more of the mysterious geometric patterns on the stones. Much about Newgrange remains a mystery, but there is an interpretative centre at the site which explains what has been discovered.

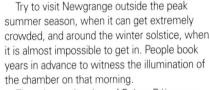

Try to visit Newgrange outside the peak summer season, when it can get extremely crowded, and around the winter solstice, when it is almost impossible to get in. People book years in advance to witness the illumination of the chamber on that morning.

The other major sites of Brú na Bóinne are the two burial chambers at **Knowth,** northwest of Slane, and the larger site at Dowth, which can only be viewed from the road.

### Newgrange and Knowth

➕ 9F ✉ Donore, Co Meath ☎ 041 988 0300;
www.heritageireland.ie 🕒 Feb–Apr, Oct daily 9:30–5:30;
May, late Sep daily 9–6:30; Jun to mid-Sep daily 9–7;
Nov–Jan daily 9–5. Closed 23–27 Dec. Knowth: early
Apr–Oct 🖐 Varies according to site; visitor centre
inexpensive 🍴 Coffee shop (€)

# 2 Clonmacnoise

**One of the most atmospheric places in Ireland, this ancient monastic city stands in peaceful seclusion beside the River Shannon.**

In AD545 St Ciaran (or Kieran) founded a monastery in this isolated place, cut off from the rest of Ireland by the wide River Shannon and surrounding bogland, and accessible only by boat. In this remote location his monastery grew into an ecclesiastical city, the most important religious foundation of its time in Ireland, and as his burial site it became a place of pilgrimage.

Over the ensuing centuries more and more buildings were added, and the ruins we see today are the most extensive of their kind in the country, including a cathedral, eight churches which were built between the 10th and 13th centuries, two round towers, three high crosses, over 600 early Christian grave slabs, two holy wells and a 13th-century castle.

A short distance away is the beautiful Romanesque "Nun's Church", which was built by Devorgilla, wife of chieftain Tiernan O'Rourke. It was her abduction by Dermot MacMurrough, King of Leinster, that led to the conflict which resulted in the Anglo-Norman invasion of Ireland.

Clonmacnoise was also the burial place of the Kings of Connaught and of Tara, including the last High King of Ireland, Rory O'Conor, who was laid to rest here in 1198. In spite of the remoteness of its setting, Clonmacnoise was known throughout Europe as a centre of excellence in art and literature. Masterpieces of Irish craftsmanship and intricate decoration produced here include the gold and silver Crozier of Clonmacnoise and the Cross of Cong, now in the Treasury of the National Museum in Dublin (➤ 48–49), and the earliest known manuscript in the vernacular Irish, the *Book of the Dun Cow*, was produced here.

✚ 19G ✉ Shannonbridge ☎ 090 967 4195; www.heritageireland.ie ⊙ Mid-Mar to mid-May, mid-Sep to Oct daily 10–6; mid-May to mid-Sep daily 9–7; Nov to mid-Mar daily 10–5 🖉 Moderate 🍴 Coffee shop end Mar–Oct (€)

# 3 Corca Dhuibhne (The Dingle Peninsula)

**Of all the glories of the west coast, the Dingle Peninsula is the most beautiful and the most dramatic.**

The Dingle Peninsula has many attractions, but best of all is its wonderful coastal scenery, which can be appreciated from the Dingle Way long-distance footpath (49km/31 miles). Along the north coast are great sweeping bays, backed by huge brooding mountains. The south has pretty little coves and the lovely Inch

beach, and in the west is the incomparable sight of the Blasket Islands off Slea Head. After exploring the coast, the drive across the Connor Pass north from Dingle and over Brandon Mountain opens up a whole new perspective, with magnificent views down towards Brandon Bay.

Dingle (An Daingean/Daingean Uí Chúis) is the main centre, a delightful town of brightly painted houses and shops, with a picturesque harbour which still supports a working fishing fleet as well as pleasure craft. These include boat trips to see the famous friendly dolphin, Fungi, who lives near the harbour mouth. Dingle is a lively place with an annual cultural festival and regatta.

Ancient sites on The Dingle include a cliff-top Iron Age fort near Ventry, Minard Castle, above Dingle Bay, and Gallarus Oratory, a tiny church dating from around the 8th century, between

Ballyferriter and Ballynana. Nearby Kilmalkedar
Church, dating from the 12th century, contains the
Alphabet Stone, inscribed with both Roman and
ancient Irish characters.

✠ 14K ℹ️ Dingle Tourist Office, The Quay ☎ 066 915 1188

# 4 The Giant's Causeway

**www.**ntni.org.uk

**This amazing geological phenomenon, set on a coastline of outstanding beauty, is one of the wonders of the natural world.**

About 40,000 columns of basalt cluster on the shoreline here, forming stepping stones from the cliffs down to the water. Most of them are hexagonal, but some have four, five, seven or eight sides, and the tallest rise to around 12m (39ft). A similar formation can be seen on the island of Staffa, over 130km (80 miles) away, off the coast of Scotland. It's thought they were formed at the same time and may be part of the same volcanic flow.

The columns are the result of volcanic action some 60 million years ago, which caused molten basalt to seep up through the chalky bedrock. When it cooled, the rock crystallized into these regular formations, but it would be easy to believe that the blocks were stacked by some giant hand, driven on in its monumental task by the force of some great purpose.

This is what the ancient Irish believed, and who else could have completed the task but the legendary giant Finn McCool, the Ulster warrior who was said to inhabit this Antrim headland? When he once scooped up a clod of earth to throw at a rival, the place he took it from filled with water to become Lough Neagh, the largest lake in the British Isles, and the clod landed in the Irish Sea

and became the Isle of Man. According to legend, he built the Causeway so that he could cross the sea to reach the lady giant of his dreams, who lived on Staffa – a tall story in more ways than one.

The reality is equally remarkable, but whatever created the Causeway, it is a magnificent sight, particularly when approached on foot from above. There is a cliff-top path all along this stretch of coastline, which can be joined at Blackrock, 2.5km (1.5 miles) from Causeway Head, or from the **Causeway Visitor Centre.**

The Visitor Centre is on the cliff top and is a good introduction to the site. It includes an audio-visual theatre, where a 25-minute show tells the story of the formation of the Causeway. There is also an exhibition area with displays including birdlife and the legend of Finn McCool. A minibus runs from here to the Causeway at regular intervals in the summer and guided tours are available.

Beside the centre is the **Causeway School Museum,** a reconstructed 1920s schoolroom complete with learning aids and toys of the era.

✚ 9A 🚌 172 Ballycastle–Portrush; summer services 177 from Coleraine and 252 from Belfast and Larne 🚉 Portrush (11km/7 miles)
**Causeway Visitor Centre**
✉ 44 Causeway Road, Bushmills ☎ 028 2073 1855
🕐 Daily 9:30–5 🎟 Free. Moderate charge for parking and extra charge for audio-visual theatre 🍴 Tea room (£)
**Causeway School Museum**
✉ 52 Causeway Road, Bushmills ☎ 028 2073 2142
🕐 Easter, Jul–Sep daily 11–5; Oct–Jun (except Easter) Mon–Fri 2–5 🎟 Inexpensive

# 5 Kilkenny

**Narrow medieval streets and alleys linking the great castle and cathedral bear witness to Kilkenny's rich history and architectural heritage.**

Standing on a bend of the River Nore, Kilkenny is one of Ireland's most beautiful towns, with pretty little streets to explore, high-quality craft studios and an exceptional range of historic buildings.

In medieval times, the town rivalled Dublin in importance and the great **castle** here was the stronghold of the most powerful family in Ireland at the time, the Butlers, Earls and Dukes of Ormonde. Though its origins are back in Norman times, the castle was adapted over the centuries and now reflects the splendour of the 1830s, enhanced by the Butler Gallery of Contemporary Art in the former servants' quarters, the Medieval Room in the South Tower and a cultural facility.

Opposite the castle is the **Kilkenny Design Centre** (► 108), which was established in the 1960s to bring Irish craftsmanship to new heights of excellence. Not only was the centre resoundingly successful, it became the spearhead of a crafts revival that has attracted fine craft workers from all over the world. **Rothe House,** a Tudor mansion on three sides of a cobbled courtyard, is also worth a visit. Here you'll find a range of restored rooms, the city and county museum and a costume collection.

Kilkenny originally grew up around the 6th-century monastery founded by St Canice, to whom the cathedral is dedicated. Built on the site of the original monastery, it remains one of the finest 13th-century buildings in Ireland and contains

impressive monuments of black Kilkenny marble
and the Cityscope Exhibition. Beside the cathedral
is the well-preserved round tower of the original
monastery, which gives great views over the city.

✚ 20J 🚉 Kilkenny 1.5km (1 mile)
🛈 Shee Alms House, Rose Inn Street ☎ 056 775 1500

**Kilkenny Castle**
✉ The Parade ☎ 056 770 4100; www.kilkennycastle.ie
🕐 Jun–Aug daily 9–5:30; Apr–May, Sep daily 9:30–5:30;
Mar daily 9:30–5; Oct–Feb daily 9:30–4:30 (guided tours
only) 🖐 Moderate

**Kilkenny Design Centre**
✉ Castle Yard ☎ 056 772 2118; www.kilkennydesign.com
🕐 May–Dec Mon–Sat 10–7, Sun 11–7; Jan–Apr Mon–Sat
10–7 🍴 Restaurant (€)

**Rothe House**
✉ Parliament Street ☎ 056 772 2893 🕐 Apr–Oct
Mon–Sat 10:30–5, Sun 3–5; Nov–Mar Mon–Sat 10:30–4
🖐 Moderate

# 6 Muckross House

**www.**muckross-house.ie

**Among Ireland's foremost stately homes, Muckross has folk and farm museums and beautiful gardens – all within the Killarney National Park.**

When Henry Arthur Herbert, Member of Parliament for Co Kerry, built his Elizabethan-style mansion in 1843, he could not have found a more perfect site, looking out towards Muckross Lake and surrounded by wonderful scenery that was destined to become a national park. Maud Bowers Bourne was given the house as a wedding present in 1911. Her family presented the house and estate to the Irish nation in 1932 in her memory.

While the house sums up the lifestyle of the landed gentry in Victorian times, the servants' quarters have been converted into a museum of Kerry folk life, with displays and a weaver's workshop. The Muckross Craft Centre features weaving, pottery and bookbinding workshops. There is also a restaurant and gift shop. Out in the grounds, a 28ha (69-acre) farm has been constructed to show farming methods that were used before mechanization. The rare Kerry cow, a small, black, hardy animal, is being bred here in order to save the herd from extinction.

The gardens at Muckross are renowned for their beauty. Many tender and exotic species thrive in the mild climate, and there are lovely water and rock gardens. A number of nature trails of various lengths begin here, from a one-hour stroll to a 16km (10-mile) circular Heritage Trail through the most extensive natural yew woods in Europe.

🚻 15L ✉ 5km (3 miles) south of Killarney ☎ 064 667 0144 🕐 House and Gardens: Jul–Aug daily 9–7; Sep–Jun daily 9–5:30. Farm: Jun–Aug daily 10–6; May daily 1–6; late Mar–Apr, Sep–Oct Sat–Sun 1–6 ✋ House and Farm expensive; House moderate; Gardens free 🍴 Cafe (€) 🚌 From Killarney ❓ Horse-drawn jaunting cars from Killarney to the house

7

# The National Museum, Dublin

**www.**museum.ie

**Three locations in Dublin house the magnificent and varied collections and priceless treasures of the National Museum.**

The oldest of the trio (1857) is the Natural History Museum, Merrion Street, known locally as the "Dead Zoo", which has one of the finest zoological collections in the world. The ground floor has collections relating to native Irish wildlife, while the upper floor has the World Collection, with many African and Asian species, all overlooked by the

skeleton of a 20m (65ft) whale. Here, too, is a wonderful collection of glass reproductions of marine specimens.

The Kildare Street branch has the archaeological collections. The centrepiece is a glittering display of ancient gold dating from around 2200 to 700BC. Some has faint traces of Celtic decoration, but the best examples of this are to be found in the National Treasury in the adjacent room. Some of the patterns, worked in silver and gold centuries ago, are almost too tiny to be appreciated by the naked eye. There is a huge collection of Viking artefacts, many found during the redevelopment of Wood Quay. The Road to Independence is an evocative exhibition on the events and consequences of the Easter Rising and the Civil War.

Across the city, on the north bank of the River Liffey, the restored Collins Barracks in Benburb Street house the National Museum's collection of decorative arts, and displays relating to social, political and military history. These include costumes and jewellery, weaponry and furniture, silver, ceramics and glassware, and interactive multimedia terminals provide more interpretation. There is also an interesting section explaining how the museum goes about the process of research, restoration and conservation of its treasures.

➕ *Dublin 8e, Dublin 1c (Decorative Arts)* ✉ Kildare Street, Merrion Street, Benburb Street ☎ 01 677 7444 🕐 Tue–Sat 10–5, Sun 2–5 🎟 Free 🍴 Cafés at Kildare Street and Collins Barracks (€) 🚌 Cross-city buses 🚆 Pearse; Heuston (Collins Barracks); Luas: Museum ❓ Guided tours depart from the main entrance at regular intervals

# 8 Oileáin Árann (Aran Islands)

**Bleak and virtually treeless, these three remote islands on the very edge of Europe have a fascinating cultural heritage.**

From the mainland, the distant sight of the three Aran Islands is mysterious and inviting. The west coast of Ireland may seem a remote outpost of Europe, and yet here is something beyond – a place where Gaelic is still the first language, old traditions live on and a small population still scratches a living from the often inhospitable land. Summer visitors are important to the economy, as is the sale of Aran knitwear.

Of the three islands – Inis Mór (Inishmore), Inis Meáin (Inishmaan) and Inis Oírr (Inisheer) – Inis Mór is the largest, and Cill Rónáin (Kilronan) is its main settlement. **Aran's Heritage Centre,** with exhibitions, crafts and an audio-visual show, will steer you towards the many attractions of the islands, from their wonderful beaches to the plentiful historic sites.

There is evidence of prehistoric settlement on the islands. Inis Mór has no fewer than five stone forts, including the dramatic Dún Aonghasa, perched above a 91m (298ft) drop to the sea, and Dún Eochla on the island's highest point.

More atmospheric still are the early Christian sites. The islands have a number of ancient churches, including Teampall Bheanáin, which was built in the 6th century, and Teampall Chiaráin, dating from the 8th or 9th centuries.

The islands deserve more than just a day trip, which can only scratch the surface of what they have to offer.

✚ 15G ⊟ No public transport on the islands ✖ Aer Arann (091-593034; www.aerarannislands.ie) operates flights taking 10 minutes from Connemara Airport, Co Galway. May–Aug every 30 mins (last flight 7pm); Sep–Apr less frequent ⛴ Island Ferries (091-568903; www.aranislandferries.com) operates several sailings daily from Rossaveal, Co Galway

**Aran's Heritage Centre**

✉ Kilronan, Inis Mór ☎ 099 61355 ◷ Jun–Aug daily 10–7; Apr–May, Sep–Oct daily 11–5 💷 Inexpensive

# 9 The Rock of Cashel

**Ancient seat of the kings of Munster and a medieval religious centre, the Rock of Cashel is an awe-inspiring sight.**

This single craggy hill, rising out of the surrounding plain and topped by a cluster of wonderful medieval buildings, dominates the skyline. It is a great landmark that draws more than the eye – its romantic outline of ruined towers and graceful arches seems to beckon from a distance.

The great rock was the obvious choice as the fortress of the kings of Munster, who ruled the southern part of Ireland, and Cashel came to prominence in the 4th or 5th century AD. Legend has it that St Patrick came here to baptize the king, and that during the ceremony, the saint accidentally

drove the sharp end of his crozier through the king's foot. The king bore the pain unflinchingly because he believed it to be part of the initiation.

The dominant building on the rock is the 13th-century St Patrick's Cathedral, roofless now, but still impressive, with its long nave and chancel and a 26m (85ft) tower. Inside is a wealth of monuments, including important tombs, and the west end is formed by a 15th-century castle, built as the Archbishop's residence.

The Round Tower and Cormac's Chapel are the oldest structures on the Rock, dating from the 11th to 12th centuries, and the chapel contains a remarkable stone sarcophagus carved with sophisticated Celtic patterns. One of the later buildings, the 15th-century Hall of the Vicars, is one of the first you see on the Rock, with a display of stone carvings in its vaulted undercroft and above it a splendid hall with a minstrels' gallery, huge fireplace and wonderful timbered ceiling.

🚉 19J 🖂 Rock of Cashel ☎ 062 61437; www.heritageireland.ie 🕐 Mid-Mar to mid-Jun daily 9:30–5:30; mid-Jun to mid-Sep daily 9–7; mid-Sep to mid-Oct daily 9–5:30; mid-Oct to mid-Mar daily 9–4:30 💶 Moderate 🚌 Dublin–Cork buses ❓ Guided tours on request. Audio-visual, Jun–Sep

# 10 Ulster American Folk Park

**www.**folkpark.com

**The lives and experiences of Ulster emigrants to the New World are authentically recreated at this splendid open-air museum.**

In a great tide of emigration during the 18th and 19th centuries, over 2 million people left Ulster for a different life in the New World. Among them was five-year-old Thomas Mellon, who went on to become a judge and founder of the Pittsburgh dynasty of bankers, and it is around his childhood home that this museum has been created. Buildings have been reconstructed on the site, giving a complete picture of the world that the emigrants left behind and the one that was awaiting them on the other side of the Atlantic.

The Ulster section includes a typical one-room cottage of the late 18th century, a forge and weaver's cottage, schoolhouse and post office, places of worship and a 19th-century street of shops, with original Victorian shopfronts. Houses include the boyhood homes of John Joseph Hughes, the first Roman Catholic Archbishop of New York, and Robert Campbell, who became a fur trader in the Rockies and a successful merchant in St Louis.

On the dockside, you can see a typical merchant's office and a boarding house where

emigrants would await their sailing, then board a reconstruction of the kind of sailing ship which carried them to their new lives.

Beyond this you emerge into the American section of the park, with log houses and barns, including a replica of the six-roomed farmhouse that Thomas Mellon's father built. The buildings contain over 2,000 19th-century artefacts collected in Pennsylvania and Virginia.

✚ 8C ✉ 2 Mellon Road, Castletown, Omagh, Co Tyrone ☎ 028 8224 3292 🕒 Apr–Sep Mon–Sat 10:30–6, Sun and public hols 11–6:30; Oct–Mar Mon–Fri 10:30–5. Last admission 90 mins before closing ✋ Moderate 🍴 Cafe (£) 🚌 273 Belfast–Londonderry ❓ Special events to celebrate the Ulster American connection are held throughout the year. Special celebrations on Independence Day, 4 July

# Best things to do

# Good places to have lunch

### Ahernes (€€–€€€)

Ahernes is a luxurious town house hotel with a restaurant that enjoys a world reputation for its fine seafood dishes.

✉ 163 North Main Street, Youghal, Co Cork ☎ 024 92424; www.ahernes.net

### Eccles Hotel (€€)

Charming Victorian hotel, where good food can be enjoyed while overlooking Bantry Bay.

✉ Glengarriff, Co Cork ☎ 027 63003

### Eden (€€–€€€)

Smart restaurant in the heart of Temple Bar, serving excellent modern Irish cuisine.

✉ Meeting House Square, Temple Bar, Dublin ☎ 01 670 5372; www.edenrestaurant.ie

### Farmgate Café (€–€€)

An informal but delicious and atmospheric lunch spot in Cork's covered English Market. A real gem.

✉ English Market, Cork ☎ 021 427 8134

### Harvey's Point (€€)

Great food in a wonderful location on the edge of Lough Eske.

✉ Lough Eske, Co Donegal ☎ 074 972 2208

### Market Bar (€–€€)

Excellent tapas in a cavernous old warehouse. WiFi throughout.

✉ Fade Street, Dublin ☎ 01 613 9094

### Nick's Warehouse (£–££)

Superb food in a popular, modern venue. The daily changing menu is dedicated to local and organic producers.

✉ 35–39 Hill Street, Belfast ☎ 028 9043 9690

### Paddy Burke's (€€)

Paddy Burke's is famous as the focal point of the popular Clarenbridge Oyster Festival, so it is not surprising that its speciality dish is shellfish.

✉ Clarenbridge, Co Galway ☎ 091 796226

### Patrick Guilbaud (€€€)

One of the finest restaurants in the city offering superb classic French cuisine in elegant surroundings, featuring a fine collection of Irish art. Popular with business clients.

✉ 21 Upper Merrion Street, Dublin ☎ 01 676 4192

### Ramore Wine Bar (£–££)

A popular restaurant right on Portrush Harbour, offering excellent food and a good wine list.

✉ The Harbour, Portrush, Co Antrim ☎ 028 7082 4313

# Best castles

**Carrickfergus Castle, Co Antrim** Built in 1180, this was one of the first, and largest, of the Irish castles (► 168). ✚ 10C

**Castle Leslie, Co Monaghan** Winston Churchill, W B Yeats, Paul McCartney – they have all fallen for the charms of this 1870 palace, now a hotel, on the shores of Glaslough Lake. ✚ 8D

**Dublin Castle, Dublin** For centuries the seat of British rule in Ireland, this stern castle sits in the heart of the capital and houses the fabulous Chester Beatty Library (► 82). ✚ *Dublin 5e*

**Johnstown Castle, Co Wexford** This Gothic Revival extravaganza was built at the heart of some magnificent parkland (► 99). ✚ 22K

**Kilkenny Castle, Co Kilkenny** Gothic and Victorian styles meet in this pristine, grey-stone castle on the banks of the River Nore in Kilkenny City (► 44–45). ✚ 20J

**Lismore Castle, Co Waterford** This vast, turreted, grey-stone building tops a rock that overhangs the Blackwater River. ✚ 19K

**Ross Castle, Killarney, Co Kerry** A splendid medieval fortress overlooking Lough Leane in Killarney National Park (► 123). ✚ 15K

**Slane Castle, Co Meath** More stately home than granite fortress, 18th-century Slane Castle overlooks a natural amphitheatre. ✚ 9F

**Trim Castle, Trim, Co Meath** The largest Anglo-Norman castle in Ireland, the de Lacys' vast stronghold was used in Mel Gibson's epic *Braveheart*. ✚ 8F

**Tullynally Castle, Co Westmeath**
The largest Irish castle still functioning as a family home. The real joy is the beautiful gardens and parkland that surround it. ✚ 7F

# Stunning scenery

Glendalough (➤ 92–93)

The Glens of Antrim (➤ 172)

The Mountains of Mourne (➤ 177)

The Ring of Kerry (➤ 122)

The Wicklow Mountains (➤ 102)

# Top activities

**Birdwatching** More than 420 different species of bird have been identified in Ireland and there are some internationally important roosting sites around Dublin Bay, Wexford and in the west.
**Bird Watch Ireland** ✉ Unit 20, Block D, Bullford Business Camp, Kilcoole, Co Wicklow ☎ 02 281 9878; www.birdwatchireland.ie

**Cruising** The Shannon–Erne waterway links the Republic's largest river to the north's finest lakes, connecting a vast network for idyllic cruising.
**Waterways Ireland** ✉ 2 Sligo Road, Enniskillen, Co Fermanagh ☎ 028 6632 3004; www.waterwaysireland.org

**Cycling** With miles of quiet country lanes and a few exciting mountain bike trails, Ireland is great for cycling. The cities, too, are manageable, with the DublinBike scheme a great innovation.
**Irish Cycle Hire** ✉ Glack, Ardee, Co Louth ☎ 041 685 3772; www.irishcyclehire.com

**Fishing** Whether it's canalside angling, sea fishing, or just catching your own fish for tea, there is fishing for all tastes in Ireland
**Central Fisheries Board** ✉ Swords Business Camp, Swords, Co Dublin ☎ 01 884 2600; www.cfb.ie

**Golf** There are more than 400 courses in Ireland, including the internationally renowned K-Club in Co Kildare. Failte Ireland and the Golf Union of Ireland produce comprehensive guides.
**Golf Union of Ireland** ✉ Carton Demesne, Maynooth, Co Kildare ☎ 01 505 4000; www.gui.ie

**Horseback riding** The affinity between the Irish and horses is legendary, and there are hundreds of places around the country where you can enjoy lovely scenery on horseback.
**Association of Irish Riding Establishments** (AIRE) ✉ Beech House, Millennium Park, Naas, Co Kildare ☎ 045 854518; www.aire.ie

**Sailing** The coast of this fantastic island is perfect for sailing, whether it's gently tacking up an inlet or rounding a challenging Atlantic headland. The Irish Sailing Association can help you find a local club or advise on safety requirements.
**Irish Sailing Association** ✉ 3 Park Road, Dun Laoghaire, Co Dublin
☎ 01 280 0239; www.sailing.ie

**Spectator sports** The Irish are passionate about sport, especially horse racing and the Gaelic games unique to the island – hurling and Gaelic football, with their spiritual home at Dublin's Croke Park.
**Gaelic Athletic Association (GAA)** ✉ Croke Park Stadium, Dublin
☎ 01 836 3222; www.gaa.ie

**Walking** Every region of Ireland offers great walking opportunities. Whether it's hillwalking in the Mournes, the Wicklows or Magillycuddy's Reeks, or on the coastal paths of Donegal or the Causeway Coast, there is plenty to choose from. Walking festivals such as Kenmare's are a popular way to explore a specific area.
☎ www. discoverireland.ie/walking.aspx

# Great boat trips

One of the best ways to see the diversity of coast, island and river scenery is to go on a boat trip. Contact the booking offices of the following companies directly or check with the local tourist office. Most trips are May to October only.

**Báan Daingin (Dingle Bay) and Fungi the Dolphin** Dingle Bay Ferries, Dunromen, Lispole, Co Kerry ☎ 066 915 1344; www.dinglebayferries.com

**Cork Harbour from Cobh** Marine Transport Services, Westland House, Rushbrooke, Cobh, Co Cork  021 481 1549

**Killarney Lakes from Ross Castle** Killarney Watercoach Cruises, Old Weir Lodge, Killarney, Co Kerry ☎ 064 663 5593

**Lough Corrib and Inchagoill Island** Tourist office, Eyre Square, Galway, Co Galway ☎ 091 537700

**Lough Derg–Killaloe** Derg Marine, Kilaloe, Co Clare ☎ 061 376364

**Lough Key Forest Park** Lough Key Boat Tours, Rockingham Harbour, Lough Key Forest Park, Boyle, Co Roscommon ☎ 086 816 7637

**Lough Ree–Athlone** Athlone Cruiser, Jolly Mariner, Marina, Athlone, Co Westmeath ☎ 090 647 2892

**River Erne from Belturbet** Emerald Star, Belturbet, Co Cavan ☎ 071 962 7633

**Skelligs from Valentia** The Skellig Experience, Valentia Island, Co Kerry ☎ 066 947 6306

**Waterford–Carrick-on-Suir Castle** Gallery Cruising Restaurant, Bridge Quay, New Ross, Co Wexford ☎ 051 421723

# Best shopping

**Aran knitwear** The distinctively patterned traditional Aran sweaters are still produced in the Oileáin Árann (Aran Islands).
**Cleo** ➤ 108

**Belleek pottery** The famous basket-weave pottery has been made at the west end of Loch Erne in Co Fermanagh since 1857 and the same traditional methods are still employed.
**Belleek Pottery Visitor Centre** ✉ 3 Main Street, Belleek, Co Fermanagh
☎ 028 6865 9300; www.belleek.ie

**Claddagh rings** Found in shops throughout Ireland, the Claddagh ring consists of a heart encircled by a pair of hands with a crown above the heart. It symbolizes love and fidelity.
**Thomas Dillon** ✉ 1 Quay Street, Galway, Co Galway ☎ 091 566365;
www.claddaghring.ie

**Connemara marble** Marble has been quarried in Connemara for centuries, and you can buy a huge range of items, from kitchen worktops to rosary beads.
**Connemara Marble Industries** ✉ Moycullen, Co Galway ✉ 091 555102

**Donegal tweed** Magee & Co in Donegal town have been manufacturing tweed since 1866.
**Magee and Co** ✉ The Diamond, Donegal, Co Donegal ☎ 074 972 2660; www.mageeireland.com

**Irish drinks** Choose from Bushmills, Jameson, Powers and Paddy whiskeys; Guinness, Beamish and Murphy's stout; Smithwick's beer; Cork gin; and Bailey's liqueur.
**Celtic Whiskey Shop** ✉ 27–28 Dawson Street, Dublin ☎ 01 675 9744; www.celticwhiskeyshop.com

**Irish lace** Irish lace-making began as a cottage industry and today is big business. Localized styles include Limerick, Kenmare, Youghal and Carrickmacross.
**Sheelin Antique Irish Lace Shop** ✉ Bellanaleck, Enniskillen, Co Fermanagh ☎ 028 6634 8052; www.irishlacemuseum.com

**Irish linen** Banbridge, Co Down is the main centre. The Ferguson Linen Centre has factory tours, and Banbridge is the starting point of Linen Tours, a coach journey around nearby sites, including linen mills and factories. There is also an Irish Linen Centre in Lisburn.
**Thomas Ferguson Irish Linen** ✉ 54 Scarva Road, Banbridge, Co Down ☎ 028 4062 3491; www.fergusonirishlinen.com

**Peat carvings** Buy a unique souvenir crafted from 5,000-year-old Irish turf from some of Ireland's oldest boglands. Choose from jewellery in traditional Celtic designs, clocks, paperweights and more. One producer is Island Turf Crafts in Coalisland, Co Tyrone.
**Island Turf Crafts** ✉ Coalisland Enterprise Centre, Unit 25, 51 Dungannon Road, Coalisland, Co Tyrone ☎ 028 8774 9041; www.islandturfcrafts.com

**Waterford crystal** The famous company went into receivership in 2009 but a new visitor centre opened a year later, and craftspeople still produce the crystal on site on a small scale (▶ 128).

# Places to take the children

### BALLYPOREEN, CO TIPPERARY
**Mitchelstown Cave**
The caves are renowned for their depth of 1km (half a mile), and comprise two groups, Desmond's Cave and New Cave.
✉ Off the M8, 4km (2.5 miles) north of Ballyporeen ☎ 052 746 7246; www.mitchelstowncave.com 🕐 Apr–Sep daily 10–5:30; Oct–Mar daily from10am – closing time varies 🖐 Moderate

### BELFAST
**Belfast Zoo**
A modern, world-class zoo set in attractive parkland and housing over 140 species of rare and endangered animals.
✉ Off Antrim Road ☎ 028 9077 6277; www.belfastzoo.co.uk 🕐 Apr–Sep daily 10–7; Oct–Mar daily 10–4 🖐 Moderate 🍴 Refreshments (£)

### W5
An interactive discovery centre at the Odyssey in central Belfast. There are five exhibition areas: Start, Go, See, Do and Discover.
✉ 2 Queen's Quay ☎ 028 9046 7700; www.w5online.co.uk 🕐 Jul–Aug daily 10–6; Sep–Jun Mon–Thu 10–5, Fri–Sat 10–6, Sun 12–6. Last entry 1 hour before closing 🖐 Moderate

### BUSHMILLS
**Giant's Causeway and Bushmills Railway**
Following the historic tram route from Bushmills to the Giant's Causeway, this is a novel approach to the World Heritage Site.
☎ 028 2073 2844 🕐 Jul–Aug daily 11–5:30; Easter–Jun, Sep–Oct Sat–Sun 11–5:30 🖐 Moderate

### DINGLE, CO KERRY
**Dingle Oceanworld**
Underwater life galore. Watch out for the sharks!
✉ Dingle Harbour ☎ 066 915 2111; www.dingle-oceanworld.ie 🕐 Daily from 10am – closing time varies 🖐 Expensive

## DUBLIN
### Dublin Zoo
This historic zoo in Phoenix Park makes an ideal family day out.
✉ Phoenix Park ☎ 01 474 8900; www.dublinzoo.ie ⏰ Mar–Oct daily
9:30–6; Nov–Feb daily 9:30–dusk ✋ Expensive 🍴 Restaurant, cafés (€–€€)

### Viking Splash Tour
Take a tour of Dublin in an ex-World War II amphibious vehicle. It
takes in all the main city-centre sights – then heads straight into
the waters of Grand Canal Basin to finish the tour afloat.
✉ 64–65 Patrick Street ☎ 01 707 6000; www.vikingsplash.ie ⏰ Feb to mid-
Nov regular daily tours (check website or call for times) ✋ Expensive

## FOTA, CO CORK
### Fota Wildlife Park
Established by the Royal Zoological Society of Ireland, Fota Wildlife
Park's primary aim is the breeding of endangered species.
✉ 1.5km (1 mile) south of Cork Harbour ☎ 021 481 2678; www.fotawildlife.ie
⏰ Mon–Sat 10–6, Sun 11–6. Last entry 5pm ✋ Expensive

## SALTHILL, CO GALWAY
### LeisureLand
A modern pool complex with waterslides, treasure cove, tropical
beach pool and playground.
☎ 091 521455; www.leisureland.ie ⏰ Mon–Fri 8am–10pm, Sat 8–5, Sun
8–6 ✋ Moderate

## TRALEE, CO KERRY
### Aqua Dome
Tralee's wonderful waterpark has all the rides you would expect.
You can also visit the nearby Blennerville Windmill.
✉ On the Dingle road ☎ Aqua Dome: 066 712 9150 ⏰ Aqua Dome Jul–Aug
daily 10–10; Sep–Jun Mon–Fri 10–10, Sat–Sun 11–8; windmill Apr–Oct
9:30–5 ✋ Expensive

# Best traditional music

Some of the best traditional music nights are the impromptu sessions in local pubs throughout Ireland. Check at the tourist offices for what's on where. Here are a few suggestions.

**Abbey Tavern** A short DART trip out of Dublin you'll find traditional music here, in the popular fishing village of Howth.
✉ 28 Abbey Street, Howth ☎ 01 839 0307 ⊕ Music usually Thu–Sat

### An Droichead Beag
A wealth of musical talent can be heard here, in the heart of the Dingle Peninsula (► 135).
✉ Main Street, Dingle ☎ 066 915 723 ⊕ Music every night

### An Spailpín Fánach
Local music students play at this popular pub (► 135).
✉ South Main Street, Cork ☎ 021 427 7949 ⊕ Music most nights

### The Cobblestone
An authentic and popular venue for traditional music.
✉ 77 North King Street, Smithfield, Dublin ☎ 01 872 1799 ⊕ Music most nights

### Crowley's
There's a tradition of good Irish music in this attractive little town in Co Kerry, and Crowley's is one of the best venues (► 135).
✉ Henry Street, Kenmare ☎ 064 664 1472 ⊕ No set times

### Fureys
One of Sligo's top venues for live music.
✉ Bridge Street, Sligo ☎ 028 9023 3768 ⊕ Check www.facebook.com

### Gus O'Connor's
This hot spot in Co Clare hosts some great music. Most of the great names have played here.

✉ Fisher Street, Doolin, Co Clare ☎ 065 707 4168 🕔 Music most nights in summer

### John Hewitt Bar
This Belfast bar hosts regular traditional music sessions, as well as some nights of jazz (▶ 185).
✉ 51 Donegall Street, Belfast ☎ 028 9023 3768 🕔 Music most nights

### Tigh Neachtain
Western Ireland is known for its great music, and this Galway institution is a great place to come and hear it.
✉ Cross Street, Galway ☎ 091 56820; www.tighneachtain.com 🕔 Music nights vary but usually Sun from 9:30pm

### Matt Molloy's
This pub is owned by Molloy, the flute player of the world-famous folk band the Chieftains.
✉ Bridge Street, Westport, Co Mayo ☎ 098 26655 🕔 Music every night from 9:30pm

# a walk

## around Dublin

**This walk starts in Dublin's most famous shopping street, then takes in many of the city's major attractions.**

*Walk south along Grafton Street, cross the road and enter the gardens of St Stephen's Green, leaving by the small gate at the left corner. Cross the road and go forward along Kildare Street.*

The National Museum, on the right, is Ireland's treasure house, with some stunning exhibits (▶ 48–49).

*At the end of Kildare Street go left into Nassau Street, then right to College Green, with Trinity College on the right (▶ 88–89). Follow Westmoreland Street, walk across O'Connell Bridge and turn left alongside the river.*

*Cross Ha'penny Bridge (footbridge), then go through Merchant's Arch into Temple Bar (▶ 88).*

This network of cobbled lanes is worth exploring.

*Turn right into Essex Street East. Take the third left into Eustace Street. At the end turn right along Dame Street.*

Dublin Castle (▶ 82) is on the left, its medieval origins buried beneath 18th-century reconstructions that house the State Apartments, including the Throne Room.

*Keep forward to Christ Church Cathedral.*

Begun in the 12th century, beautiful Christ Church is the foremost cathedral in Dublin. Next to it is Dvblinia and the Viking World (▶ 84).

*Go down Fishamble Street to the river. Turn right along the south bank, and at O'Connell Bridge turn right and return to Grafton Street.*

**Distance** About 4km (2.5 miles)
**Time** 3–4 hours
**Start/end point** Grafton Street ✚ *Dublin 7e*
**Lunch** Bad Ass Café (€), 9–11 Crown Alley, Temple Bar, tel 01 671 2596

# Great literary connections

**Roddy Doyle (born 1958)** Doyle won the Booker Prize in 1993 with *Paddy Clarke Ha Ha Ha*, but is perhaps best known for his Barrytown trilogy, set in Dublin's Northside during the 1980s recession years: *The Commitments, The Snapper* and *The Van*.
🚇 DART Killester

**Seamus Heaney (born 1939)** The Nobel laureate poet was born in Mossbawn, Co Londonderry. He graduated from Queen's University Belfast and went on to become a professor.
**Queen's University Welcome Centre** ➤ 163

**James Joyce (1882–1941)** Now one of Dublin's favourite sons, Joyce's relationship with his home town was not so rosy when he was alive. The city is awash with Joycean venues, but perhaps the most evocative is the Martello Tower at Sandycove, which hosts the opening chapter in *Ulysses*.
**James Joyce Centre** ✉ 35 Great North George's Street, Dublin ☎ 01 878 8547; www.jamesjoyce.ie

**Patrick Kavanagh (1904–67)** The poet's bronze effigy can be found gazing out over the Grand Canal near the Baggot Street Bridge, a reference to his poem *Canal Bank Walk*.
**Kavanagh statue** ✉ Grand Canal, Wilton Terrace, Dublin

**Frank McCourt (1930–2009)** The American writer's childhood in poverty-stricken Limerick was graphically described in *Angela's Ashes*. The city has changed enormously, but you can still see sites of some of the key scenes in the modern city.
**Limerick Tourist Office** ✉ Arthur's Quay, Limerick ☎ 061 317522

**George Bernard Shaw (1856–1950)** "Author of many plays" is the simple accolade on the plaque outside Shaw's birthplace, close to the Grand Canal in Portobello, Dublin.
**Shaw Birthplace** ✉ 33 Synge Street, Dublin ☎ 01 475 0854

**Jonathan Swift (1667–1745)** Best known for *Gulliver's Travels*, this satirical Dubliner was Dean of St Patrick's Cathedral from 1713 till his death. He was buried in the cathedral.
**St Patrick's Cathedral** ✉ Patrick Street, Dublin ☎ 01 453 9472

**Oscar Wilde (1854–1900)** The famous writer was born in Dublin. You can see his house (not open to the public) in Merrion Square. And opposite, don't miss the wonderfully louche reclining statue of the great man himself.
**Oscar Wilde House** ✉ Merrion Square, Dublin

**W B Yeats (1865–1939)** Though he was born in Dublin, the poet is more closely associated with other parts of Ireland. There's a statue and festival in Sligo and a museum at his one-time residence in Galway.
**Thoor Ballylee Tower** ✉ Gort, Co Galway ☎ 091 631436

# Exploring

It's the diverse nature of Ireland that lives in the memory. From vibrant, cosmopolitan cities to quiet rural backwaters; from dramatic coast to rugged mountains; from picture postcard villages to market towns – the country and its people are unique. If you have only time to visit Dublin, at least try and take a trip out of town on the DART; in a few minutes you will find yourself out along the coast, adding a further dimension to your visit. As in so many countries, the cities are only part of the whole and not a true reflection of the country. You won't go anywhere very fast, although the roads have improved dramatically, but then that is part of the charm. People don't rush in Ireland, and even in Dublin and Belfast, now cities competing with any other major European destination for culture, restaurants and vibrant nightlife, the locals still have time to stop and chat.

# Dublin and the East

**The eastern part of Ireland is inevitably dominated by Dublin, a lively city with a lot to see and do, but the east has much more to offer than just the capital. Ireland's most extensive mountain region is just to the south of Dublin in Co Wicklow, where remote, silent valleys and wild exposed mountain tops can be reached in less than half an hour's drive.**

Dublin

Long sandy beaches and golf links stretch all along the coast, which remains unspoiled in spite of the presence of the main ferry ports. Likewise, the seaside resorts retain an old-fashioned appeal.

Inland, the east has some fascinating places to see. To the north

of Dublin is a cluster of historic sites including Tara, Kells and the neolithic remains at Newgrange. Southwest of the capital is the horse-racing centre of Kildare and The Curragh and the wonderful old city of Kilkenny, while in the far south are the pretty villages and fine beaches of the Wexford coast.

## DUBLIN

Part of Dublin's charm is that it takes only a few days of wandering around its attractive streets and leafy squares to feel you know the city intimately. And yet, every visit reveals some new delight.

Dublin has everything a capital city should have – magnificent architecture, excellent shopping, great restaurants, lively entertainment and cultural events, superb museums and galleries, colourful parks and gardens and a strong sense of history.

Until now, most of Dublin's attractions have been in the smart areas south of the river. The northside was once a run-down area with seedy back streets, but now a redevelopment plan has given it the designer treatment. Wide O'Connell Street has become an attractive, leafy boulevard; behind it in Henry Street the shopping centres have been upgraded and the area is now an alternative to Grafton Street. Until the economic crisis of 2008, Smithfield was developing as an interesting cultural quarter to rival Temple Bar, but this has tailed off. The docks are being developed and the Luas light rail system brings Dubliners in from the suburbs.

✚ 22G

ℹ Suffolk Street ☎ 01 605 7700

### Dublin Castle

Soon after the Anglo-Normans arrived in Ireland in the 12th century, King John ordered the building of Dublin Castle and it remained the centre of English power in Ireland until 1922. In spite of its great medieval walls and round bastions, much of the castle is a product of the 18th century, including the State Apartments, where presidents are inaugurated and dignitaries received. The Chester Beatty Library, one of the world's best collections of Oriental and European manuscripts, is located in the castle gardens.

**www.**dublincastle.ie

✚ *Dublin 5e* ✉ Castle Street ☎ 01 677 7129 🕐 Mon–Sat 10–4:45, Sun, public hols 2–4:45 (State Apartments may be closed for functions) 🎟 Free. State Apartments tour moderate 🍴 Restaurant (€) 🚌 Cross-city buses

### Dublin Writers Museum

Few cities in the world have spawned so many writers of international repute, including four Nobel prize winners, and this museum is a celebration of that literary heritage. The displays, in the magnificent surroundings of a restored 18th-century mansion, encompass the whole spectrum of Irish works, from the 8th-century *Book of Kells* to the present, taking in Swift, Sheridan, Shaw, Wilde, Yeats, Joyce and Beckett along the way.

One room is devoted entirely to children's literature, and there are regular exhibitions and readings.

**www.**writersmuseum.com

✚ *Dublin 6a* ✉ 18–19 Parnell Square North ☎ 01 872 2077 ⏰ Mon–Sat 10–5, Sun and public hols 11–5 ✋ Moderate 🍴 Restaurant (€€) and coffee shop (€) 🚌 10, 11, 11A, 11b, 13, 16A, 19a, 22, 22A, 36 🚇 DART and Luas: Connolly

### Dvblinia and the Viking World

Developed by the Medieval Trust, Dvblinia tells the story of the city from the arrival of the Anglo-Normans in the 12th century until the closure of the monasteries in 1540. It is housed in a beautifully preserved old building, the former Synod Hall, linked to Christ Church Cathedral by an ancient covered bridge. The "Viking World" exhibition reconstructs life in even earlier Viking Dublin.
**www.**dublinia.ie

✚ *Dublin 4e* ✉ St Michael's Hill ☎ 01 679 4611 ⏱ Daily 10–4:30
⚑ Moderate 🍴 Tea rooms Easter–Aug (€) 🚌 51B, 78A, 90, 123

### Guinness Storehouse

Guinness, one of the most potent symbols of Irishness, is now brewed all over the world – at a rate of over 10 million glasses a day – and this is where it all started, founded by Arthur Guinness in 1759. As you enter the Storehouse through a stone arch an

escalator whisks you to the heart of the building into what is best described as a large glass pint. Within this glass structure you journey through the production process. Entertaining displays and audio-visuals give an insight into the history, manufacturing and advertising of Dublin's most famous product. You will end your visit in the glass-walled rooftop bar where you can sample a free glass of the "black stuff".

**www**.guinness-storehouse.com

➕ *Dublin 1e* ✉ St James's Gate ☎ 01 408 4800 🕐 Daily 9:30–5, (until 7pm Jul–Aug) 🖐 Expensive 🍴 Brewery bar, Gravity bar 🚌 51B, 78A from Aston Quay; 123 from O'Connell Street. Luas: James's

## Kilmainham Gaol

In its time both a caution and an inspiration, Kilmainham Gaol stands as a monument to the struggle for Irish independence and those leaders of the 1916 Easter Rising who were imprisoned or executed here. It gives visitors a chillingly realistic impression of what life must have been like for the prisoners who were incarcerated here, be they patriots or petty criminals, from its inauguration in 1796 to 1924.

➕ *Dublin 1d (off map)* ✉ Inchicore Road, Kilmainham ☎ 01 453 5984; www.heritageireland.ie 🕐 Apr–Sep daily 9:30–6; Oct–Mar Mon–Sat 9:30–5:30, Sun 10–6. Last tour 1 hour before closing 🖐 Moderate 🚌 51B, 78A, 79 from Aston Quay. Luas: Suir Road 🚆 Heuston

### National Gallery of Ireland

First opened in 1864, this wonderful gallery has one of the finest collections of European art in the world. Located in the heart of Georgian Dublin, the gallery contains nearly 2,500 paintings, over 5,000 drawings, watercolours and miniatures, over 3,000 prints and more than 300 pieces of sculpture and objets d'art. The Millennium Wing houses a centre for the study of Irish art and an archive dedicated to the paintings of Jack B Yeats (1871–1957).

**www.**nationalgallery.ie

➕ *Dublin 8e* ✉ Merrion Square West and Clare Street ☎ 01 661 5133 ⏲ Mon–Wed, Fri–Sat 9:30–5:30, Thu 9–8:30, Sun 12–5:30 💷 Voluntary donation 🍴 Restaurant and café (€€) 🚌 Cross-city buses 🚆 DART Pearse

### The National Museum

Best places to see, ➤ 48–49.

### Old Jameson Distillery

Explore the history of Irish whiskey-making, which goes back to the 6th century, through exhibits and audio-visual presentations on the site of the old Jameson Distillery in Smithfield Village, on the north side of the River Liffey. You can view old and new equipment and watch a working bottling line, then sample a drop of the *uisce beatha*, literally "water of life". There is an excellent shop selling a variety of whiskies, as well as clothing and posters.

**www.**jamesonwhiskey.com

✚ *Dublin 3c* ✉ Bow Street, Smithfield
☎ 01 807 2355 ◷ Daily 9:30–6 (last tour 5:30), guided tours only, every 30 mins
✋ Expensive 🍴 Restaurant and bar
(€–€€) 🚌 68, 69, 79, 90. Luas: Smithfield

### St Patrick's Cathedral

The national cathedral of the protestant Church of Ireland, St Patrick's is arguably the most beautiful religious building in the country. Legend has it that Patrick baptized converts at a well here. The original Early English Gothic-style building was dedicated in 1192. At 93m (305ft), it is the longest church in the country, a property Oliver Cromwell found useful when he used the nave to stable his cavalry's horses in the 17th century, incidentally leaving it in an awful state. The Guinness family paid for much of the original restoration over a hundred years ago. The most famous of St Patrick's deans, the satirical genius Jonathan Swift, has his tomb in the south aisle.

**www.**stpatrickscathedral.ie

✚ *Dublin 4f* ✉ Patrick's Street, Dublin 2 ☎ 01 453 9472 ◷ Mar–Oct daily 9–5:30; Nov–Feb Mon–Sat 9–5, Sun 9–3 ✋ Moderate 🚌 51B, 78A, 90, 123

### Temple Bar

Sooner or later, every visitor to Dublin heads to the area known as Temple Bar, a lively warren of narrow, cobbled streets just south of the Liffey. It gets its name from Anglo-Irish Sir William Temple, who bought the land in the 16th century. There is access from all sides, but the best way in is to walk across the Ha'penny Bridge from the north side of the river and keep straight on through the arch.

You'll find every kind of watering hole and eating place here, from super-touristy pubs like the Oliver St John Gogarty (58–59 Fleet Street; go for the Sunday brunch music session) to bistros and cafés. There are galleries, pubs, buskers and music just about everywhere.

➕ Dublin 6d

### Trinity College

Through the Palladian facade of Trinity College is not only an oasis of peace and quiet in the heart of the busy city centre, but also one of Dublin's finest ranges of buildings.

The college was founded in 1592 by Elizabeth I, and has many fine buildings from the 18th and 19th centuries. The finest of them all is the **Old Library** (1732), which contains some of Ireland's greatest treasures. Magnificent illuminated manuscripts on display include the 9th-century *Book of Kells* and the *Book of Armagh*.

The main entrance is on College Street, opposite the Bank of Ireland, next to one of the busiest roads in Dublin. On Parliament Square, inside the college grounds, you will find the 19th-century campanile and the elegant 18th-century Dining Hall and the Chapel.
**www.tcd.ie**
✚ *Dublin 7d*

**Old Library**
✉ College Street ☎ College: 01 896 1000. Old Library: 01 896 2320 🕙 Old Library: Mon–Sat 9:30–5, Sun 12:30–4:30 (from 9:30 Jun–Sep). Closed 10 days at Christmas 💷 Campus free; Library and *Book of Kells* expensive 🚌 Cross-city buses

## The East

### BRÚ NA BÓINNE
Best places to see, ➤ 36–37.

### CASTLETOWN HOUSE
Castletown at Celbridge is Ireland's largest and finest Palladian country house, built in the 18th century for William Connolly, Speaker of the Irish House of Commons. The central block, modelled on an Italian palazzo, is linked to its two wings with gracefully curving colonnades.

The sumptuous interiors, including the Pompeian Gallery, are largely the inspiration of Lady Louisa Lennox, who came to the house after her marriage in 1758. At its heart is a magnificent hall, with a sweeping cantilevered staircase and superb plasterwork. It's managed by the Office of Public Works.

**www**.castletown.ie

➕ 22G ✉ Celbridge, Co Kildare ☎ 01 628 8252 🕐 Easter to mid-Nov Tue–Sun 10–6 (last admission 4:45) 👤 Inexpensive 🚌 67, 67A from Wellington Quay, Dublin

### CEANANNUS MOR (KELLS)

In AD806 a Columban monastery was founded at Kells by monks who had fled the Viking raids on Iona. It was to become one of the great centres of Celtic Christianity, and it was here that the magnificently decorated version of the Gospels, the *Book of Kells*, was completed. This is now a prized possession of Dublin's Trinity College Library (➤ 88–89), after being moved there during the Cromwellian wars. Replicas are on display in the town's heritage centre, though this is currently closed.

The town's street pattern reflects the circular shape of the monastery, of which only a round tower and the tiny St Columcille's House remain. The original doorway of the house was 2.4m (8ft) above ground level, a defensive measure which reflected troubled times. Close to the round tower, in the churchyard, are three carved stone crosses, also from the 9th century. A fourth, with 30 decorative panels, stands in Market Square.

➕ 8F ✉ Tourist Information Centre, Kells Civic Offices, Headfort Place, Kells, Co Meath ☎ 046 924 0076 🕐 Mon–Fri 9–1, 2–5

## GLENDALOUGH

Deep in the heart of the Wicklow Mountains (➤ 102) are the atmospheric remains of a remarkable monastic city which was founded in the 6th century by St Kevin and remained an important place of pilgrimage well into the 18th century.

Many legends surround the mysterious St Kevin. He is said to have come to Glendalough to avoid worldly pleasures and the advances of a beautiful redheaded woman with "unholy eyes", and that he rolled himself, and his putative lover, in stinging nettles to dampen their desire. He may also have hurled the lady into an icy lake to cool her ardour.

Some of the remains, accessible only by boat, are on the south side of the Upper Lake and include the reconstructed Tempull na Skellig and St Kevin's Bed, a small cave reached after a difficult climb.

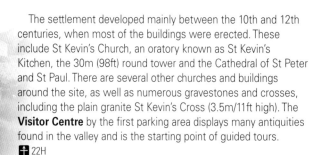

The settlement developed mainly between the 10th and 12th centuries, when most of the buildings were erected. These include St Kevin's Church, an oratory known as St Kevin's Kitchen, the 30m (98ft) round tower and the Cathedral of St Peter and St Paul. There are several other churches and buildings around the site, as well as numerous gravestones and crosses, including the plain granite St Kevin's Cross (3.5m/11ft high). The **Visitor Centre** by the first parking area displays many antiquities found in the valley and is the starting point of guided tours.

✚ 22H

### Glendalough Visitor Centre

✚ Glendalough, Bray, Co Wicklow ☎ 040-445325/445352; www.heritageireland.ie ⏰ Mid-Mar to mid-Oct daily 9:30–6; mid-Oct to mid-Mar daily 9:30–5 💷 Inexpensive 🚌 St Kevin's bus twice daily from Dublin

## IRISH NATIONAL HERITAGE PARK

On the River Slaney, a little way west of Wexford, is the Irish National Heritage Park, which recreates Irish life over a period of about 9,000 years, ending with the Anglo-Norman period. No fewer than 14 historical sites have been recreated amid the maturing woodland of the 14ha (34.5-acre) site. The trappings and paraphernalia of everyday life through the ages help to bring it all to life, and the park successfully combines the requirements of tourism with serious historical content.

✚ 21K ✉ Ferrycarrig, Co. Wexford ☎ 053-912 0733 ⏰ May–Aug daily 9:30–6:30; Sep–Apr 9:30–5:30 (last entry 3pm) 💷 Moderate 🍴 Restaurant (€€)

### JERPOINT ABBEY

Jerpoint Abbey is one of Ireland's finest monastic ruins. The first religious house here was a Benedictine abbey, founded around 1158, but by 1180 it had been taken over by the Cistercians. Substantial remains of buildings from the 12th to the 15th centuries tower above the main road. For all its size and presence, however, what is most interesting here are the amusing carvings along the restored cloister arcade, the monuments and effigies.

✚ 20J ✉ Thomastown, Co Kilkenny ☎ 056 772 4623
🕐 Jun to mid-Sep daily 10–6; mid-Sep to Oct, Mar–May daily 10–5; Nov–early Dec daily 10–4; Dec–Mar by appointment only
✋ Inexpensive

### KILDARE

This old county town has an attractive central square and some medieval buildings. St Brigid's Cathedral is on the site of a monastery founded in AD490 and nearby is a 10th-century

round tower with wonderful views. The other tower in the town is that of the 15th-century castle.

Kildare is at the heart of horse-racing country, and Irish-bred horses are among the most prized in the world. The **Irish National Stud** at Tully House gives visitors an insight into the development of these magnificent animals.

The **Japanese Gardens** at Tully House, landscaped between 1906 and 1910 by Japanese gardener Tasa Eida, include a tea house and a miniature village carved from rock from Mount Fuji. The gardens symbolize the life of man, taking the pilgrim-soul on a journey from Birth to Eternity.

**St Fiachra's Garden** seeks to recreate the landscape of rocks and water that inspired spirituality in early monastic life. At its heart is a superb bronze statue of St Fiachra, noted for his love of nature, sitting holding up a seed. A stone hermitage contains pieces of sparkling Waterford crystal representing rocks and flowers.

21G

**Irish National Stud/Japanese Gardens/St Fiachra's Garden**

Tully, Kildare 045 521617; www.irish-national-stud.ie Mid-Feb to mid-Nov daily 9:30–5:30; mid-Nov to Dec daily 9:30–5 Moderate
Restaurant (€€) Dublin–Kildare (then shuttle bus to Kildare Outlet Village shopping also stops at stud)

### KILKENNY

Best places to see, ➤ 44–45.

### MALAHIDE

The town of Malahide is a traditional seaside resort that has also become a popular residential area for commuters to Dublin. One of its great attractions is that it is particularly well endowed with good restaurants, but its main boast is the magnificent **castle.** It is one of Ireland's oldest, with a romantic medieval outline

that has changed little in its 800 years. The interior has been transformed over the centuries, and now contains superb Irish furniture and paintings, including a historic portrait collection which is, in effect, a National Portrait Gallery.

**www.**malahidecastle.com

✚ 10F

**Malahide Castle**

☎ 01-846 2184 ⏰ Apr–Sep daily 10–5; Oct–Mar Mon–Sat 10–5, Sun and public hols 11–5 🖐 Moderate 🍴 Restaurant (€€) 🚌 42 from Dublin 🚉 DART Malahide

### MONASTERBOICE

One of Ireland's best-known Christian sites, Monasterboice was founded by St Buite in the 6th century and thrived for 600 years, until the new Cistercian Mellifont Abbey superseded it in importance. The site includes a remarkable 10th-century round tower which stands 33m (108ft) high (without its roof) and
offers a good view of the encircling ramparts. There are also three superb high crosses, of which the South Cross (Cross of Muiredach) is the best, a 6m (19.5ft) monolith with distinctive sculptural detail of biblical scenes, including Eve tempting Adam, Cain murdering Abel and Judgement Day. The West Cross is the tallest, with some expressive carving, but has suffered from erosion. The North Cross has a plain, modern shaft.

✚ 9E ✉ Near Drogheda, Co Louth ⏰ Always accessible 🖐 Free 🍴 Forge Gallery Restaurant (€€€), Collon, tel 041 982 6272

## POWERSCOURT HOUSE AND GARDENS

Amid the wild landscape of the Wicklow Mountains
(➤ 102) is one of the most superb gardens in Europe.
Powerscourt Gardens were originally laid out in the
mid-17th century to complement the magnificent
Powerscourt House. Great formal terraces step down
the south-facing slope, with distinctive mosaics of
pebbles (taken from the beach at Bray). There are
beautiful lakes and fountains, statues and decorative
ironwork, American, Italian and Japanese gardens and, in contrast,
charming kitchen gardens and a little pet cemetery. Avid gardeners
who are inspired by all the beauty can visit the Pavilion garden
centre and take a little piece of it home.

In every direction is a backdrop of mountain peaks, and Ireland's
highest waterfall plunges 121m (397ft) into a picturesque valley
within the park. The Glen of the Dargle is a wooded gorge, dotted
with modern sculpture. More than 20 years after it was destroyed
by fire, Powerscourt House reopened its doors. It houses an
exhibition about its history, which includes a visit to the former
ballroom, an excellent gallery of shops and a terrace café.
**www.**powerscourt.ie

🚩 22G ✉ Enniskerry, Co Wicklow ☎ 01 204 6000 🕓 Daily 9:30–5:30 (dusk
in winter) 👋 Expensive 🍴 Restaurant (€–€€); kiosk at waterfall 🚆 DART to
Bray, then bus 185 to Enniskerry

## WEXFORD

With its huge natural harbour and its location close to the
southeastern point of Ireland, over the centuries Wexford was
the natural landing place for travellers from Wales, Cornwall and
France. The Vikings were the first settlers in the 9th or 10th
century, and the narrow lanes that cluster behind the waterfront
are a legacy of those far-off times. Wexford was also the first Irish
settlement to fall to the invading Anglo-Normans in 1169, and soon
afterwards, at Selskar Abbey, the Anglo-Irish treaty was signed.

Wexford is an interesting mixture of working county town, with busy streets, lively pubs and a famous opera festival, and historic Heritage Town, with some of its 14th-century town wall still intact. The four-storey West Gate houses the Heritage Centre, with an audio-visual presentation about the town.

The nearby mudflats known as The Slobs are now the Wexford Wildfowl Reserve, with a research station, a visitor centre, hides (camouflaged shelters) and a lookout tower. The reserve is of international importance, having one-third of the world's population of Greenland white-fronted geese.

Close by is Johnstown Castle, home of the **Irish Agricultural Museum,** housed in historic farm buildings.

🚩 22K

### Irish Agricultural Museum

✉ Johnstown Castle ☎ 053 917 1247; www.irishagrimuseum.ie 🕐 Apr–Oct Mon–Fri 9–5, Sat–Sun and public hols 11–4:30; Nov–Mar Mon–Fri 9–5 ✋ Moderate 🍴 Coffee shop, Jul–Aug (€)

# a drive

## around the Wicklow Mountains

**This drive includes the beautiful Wicklow Mountains, two of Ireland's finest gardens and the monastic remains at Glendalough.**

*Leave Wicklow on the Dublin road and continue to Ashford.*

Mount Usher Gardens, off to the right along the banks of the River Vartry, are a superb example of "wild gardens".

*In Ashford turn left, then fork right, following signs for Roundwood. At the T-junction by Roundwood church, turn left, then fork right, signposted Enniskerry. Continue, following signs for Enniskerry.*

The entrance to Powerscourt House and Gardens is on a bend at the start of the village. The gardens are among the finest in Europe, and Powerscourt Waterfall is Ireland's highest.

*In Enniskerry, turn left, and after 8km (5 miles) reach Glencree. At the next junction head for Sally Gap, Glendalough. After another*

*8km (5 miles) turn right, and keep following signs for Blessington until you reach the N81. Turn left. After 3km (2 miles) turn left onto the R758 signposted Valleymount, Lake Drive. Continue, on the R756, following signs for Glendalough.*

This interesting ancient settlement is one of Ireland's major attractions, with atmospheric ruins.

*Return to the junction on the R756 and go on through Laragh. After 5km (3 miles) turn right, signposted Arklow, Rathdrum R755. In Rathdrum follow signs for Avoca. At the T-junction, turn left, then bear right, signposted Dublin. After 13km (8 miles) turn right to return to Wicklow.*

**Distance** 117km (73 miles)
**Time** About 5–6 hours, depending on attractions visited
**Start/end point** Wicklow ✚ 23H
**Lunch** Powerscourt Terrace Café (€), Powerscourt House, tel 01 204 6070

## THE WICKLOW MOUNTAINS

Just a short distance from the centre of Dublin (➤ 82–89) is this wonderfully secluded area of high mountains and peaceful valleys. Lugnaquilla is the highest point, at 925m (3,035ft), and is the source of the River Slaney. Two scenic passes cross the mountains from east to west – the Sally Gap on the old Military Road and the Wicklow Gap further south.

Great forests clothe many of the mountain slopes, including Coollatin Park near Shillelagh, in the south, which preserves remnants of the oak forests which are said to have supplied the roof timbers for Dublin's St Patrick's Cathedral and London's Palace of Westminster. Near Blessington is the great Pollaphuca Reservoir, providing Dublin with both water and electricity, with scenic lakeside drives and good fishing.

Signs of historic habitation include ancient hill forts and stone circles, the monastic site at Glendalough (➤ 92–93) and the mansions of Powerscourt at Enniskerry (➤ 98) and Russborough House, near Blessington. More sinister associations are attached to the creepy ruin of the Hell Fire Club on top of Mount Pelier near Tallaght. Ask the locals to tell you its story, then climb up (in daylight!) for a look. The views are wonderful.

✚ 22H ⑪ Johnnie Fox's Pub (€€; ➤ 106)

## HOTELS

### AVOCA, CO WICKLOW

**Sheepwalk House (€)**

A cosy 18th-century house 3km (2 miles) from Avoca, with lovely views over the Arklow Valley.

✉ Beech Road, Avoca ☎ 0402 35189; www.sheepwalk.com 🕒 Closed Dec–Jan

### DUBLIN, CO DUBLIN

**Charleville Lodge (€–€€)**

This highly recommended guest house is in a Victorian terrace near Phoenix Park.

✉ 268–272 North Circular Road ☎ 01 838 6633; www.charlevillelodge.ie

**Kilronan House (€€)**

Stylish Georgian house in a peaceful location close to the National Concert Hall.

✉ 70 Adelaide Road ☎ 01 475 5266; www.dublinn.com

**Maldron (€–€€)**

Overlooking the cobbled Smithfield Plaza, the Maldron is an affordable alternative to central Dublin, with ideal connections to the Luas and DublinBike.

✉ Smithfield ☎ 01 485 0900; www.maldronhotels.com

**Merrion (€€€)**

The epitome of relaxed grandeur, the Merrion, comprising four gracious Georgian town houses, has superb bedrooms and opulent bathrooms that reflect the 18th-century architecture.

✉ Upper Merrion Street ☎ 01 603 0600; www.merrionhotel.com

**Trinity Capital (€€–€€€)**

You can't miss this unusual but comfortable boutique-style hotel: it's in a converted fire station. It's conveniently within walking distance of most main attractions.

✉ Pearse Street ☎ 01 648 1000; www.trinitycapitalhotel.com

### KILKENNY, CO KILKENNY
**Butler House (€€–€€€)**

Georgian mansion with elegant interiors, restored by the Irish State Design Agency. Peaceful location, but close enough to the city centre and castle to be a good base for sightseeing.

✉ 16 Patrick Street ☎ 056 772 2828; www.butler.ie ✪ Closed 24–29 Dec

### RATHNEW, CO WICKLOW
**Hunters Hotel (€€€)**

Rambling 16th-century coaching inn has loads of character and lovely gardens running down to the river. Good restaurant featuring some excellent fish dishes.

✉ Newrath Bridge ☎ 0404 40106; www.hunters.ie

**Tinakilly Country House (€€–€€€)**

This elegant mansion is set in 3ha (7.5 acres), with sea views.

☎ 0404 69274; www.tinakilly.ie

### NAAS, CO KILDARE
**Killashee House (€€–€€€)**

Set in over 80ha (200 acres) of parkland, this opulent but friendly 141-bed spa hotel has views to the Wicklow Mountains.

☎ 045 879277; www.killasheehouse.com

## RESTAURANTS

### DALKEY, CO DUBLIN
**Guinea Pig (The Fish Restaurant) (€€€)**

Family-run restaurant with an extensive, though not exclusively, seafood-based menu.

✉ 17 Railway Road ☎ 01 285 9055 ✪ Daily from 5.30pm

### DUBLIN, CO DUBLIN
**Il Baccaro (€€)**

Intimate Italian restaurant in a 17th-century cellar in the heart of Temple Bar.

✉ Diceman's Corner ☎ 01 671 4597; www.ilbaccaro.com ✪ Thu–Sat lunch, dinner, Mon–Wed dinner

### Chapter One (€€€)

A classy gem on the Northside, this French-inspired restaurant is located in the basement of the Dublin Writers Museum.

✉ 18–19 Parnell Square North ☎ 01 873 2266 🕒 Tue–Fri 12:30–2, 6–10.30, Sat 6–10.30; closed first 2 weeks Aug

### L'Gueuleton (€–€€)

Understated French-style eatery proving excellent cuisine doesn't have to break the bank. The Toulouse sausages are particularly popular. Lunch is very good value too.

✉ 1 Fade Street ☎ 01 675 3708 🕒 Mon–Sat 12:30–3, 6–10, Sun 1–3, 6–9

### Monty's of Kathmandu (€€€)

Monty's serves good, authentic Nepalese cuisine at the Dame Street end of Eustace Street. Often sought out by visiting celebs.

✉ 22 Eustace Street, Temple Bar ☎ 01 670 4911; www.montys.ie 🕒 Mon–Sat 12–2, 5:30–11, Sun 5:30–10:30

### Nonna Valentina (€€€)

Enjoying a delightful canalside setting in Portobello, this fine Italian restaurant serves food from a precious family recipe book.

✉ 1 Portobello Road ☎ 01 454 9866; nonnavalentina.ie 🕒 Tue–Sat from 6pm, Sun from noon

### Patrick Guilbaud (€€€)

See page 59.

### Queen of Tarts (€)

Super home-made cakes and pastries. Salads and cream teas, too. All served in intimate surroundings by friendly staff.

✉ 4 Cork Hill, Dame Street ☎ 01 670 7499 🕒 Mon–Fri 8–7, Sat 9–7, Sun 10–6

## ENNISKERRY, CO WICKLOW
### Powerscourt Terrace Café (€)

Wonderful views over the Powerscourt gardens and to the mountains beyond.

✉ Powerscourt House ☎ 01-204 6070 🕐 Mon–Fri 9:30–4:30, Sat–Sun 9:30–5

## GLENCULLEN, CO DUBLIN
### Johnnie Fox's Pub (€€)
An 18th-century coaching inn known for its excellent seafood, with fresh mussels a speciality. Music and dancing nightly.
✉ Glencullen ☎ 01 295 5647 🕐 Daily 12:30–9

## GOREY, CO WEXFORD
### Marlfield House (€€€)
The restaurant at this country house hotel serves up a heady mix of classical French cuisine infused with Mediterranean flavours.
✉ Courtown Road ☎ 053 942 112 🕐 Daily 12–11:30

## GREYSTONES, CO WICKLOW
### Hungry Monk (€€€)
The place for a romantic candlelit supper overlooking a scenic golf course. Good traditional Irish dishes.
✉ Church Road ☎ 01 287 5759 🕐 Mon–Sat 5–11, Sun 12:30–9

## HOWTH, CO DUBLIN
### King Sitric Fish Restaurant (€€€)
Co Dublin's best-known fish restaurant.
✉ East Pier ☎ 01 832 5235 🕐 Wed–Sat, Mon from 6:30pm, Sun 1–7

## KILDARE, CO KILDARE
### Chapter 16 (€€)
Modern, bright new addition to the local dining scene, with a solid menu touched with moments of imagination.
✉ The Square ☎ 045 522232 🕐 Mon–Sat 6–10, Sun 5–9:30

## KILKENNY, CO KILKENNY
### Kilkenny Design Centre (€)
The restaurant at this complex of craft workshops serves traditional Irish dishes and vegetarian selections.
✉ Castle Yard ☎ 056 772 2118 🕐 Daily during shopping hours

## KILMACANOGE, CO WICKLOW
### Avoca Handweavers (€)
Set in the Wicklow Mountains and serving delicious home-cooked food. Good selection for vegetarians.
✉ Kilmacanoge ☎ 01 286 7466 🕐 Daily 9:30–5:30

## LEIGHLINBRIDGE, CO CARLOW
### The Lord Bagenal Inn (€€)
Country inn serving international and Irish cuisine in a traditional bar and restaurant.
✉ Main Street ☎ 059 977 4000 🕐 Daily 12–6. Bar meals Mon–Sat 9am–10pm, Sun 9–9

## SKERRIES, CO DUBLIN
### Stoop Your Head (€–€€)
Fresh, simple seafood packs in the discerning diners. The stoop is needed to avoid a low beam in the centre of the building.
✉ Harbour Road ☎ 01 849 2085 🕐 Mon–Sat 12:30–3, 5:30–9:30, Sun 4–8

## WEXFORD, CO WEXFORD
### The Wrens Nest (€)
A great place to meet the locals. Good bar meals.
✉ Custom House Quay ☎ 053 912 2359 🕐 Lunch Mon–Sat until 3pm

# SHOPPING

## CRAFTS
### Avoca Handweavers
The oldest working woollen mill in Ireland. All kinds of Irish-made crafts. Café.
✉ Avoca, Co Wicklow ☎ 01 286 7466 🕐 Daily 9:30–5:30

### Bogwood Sculpture Studio
Beautiful sculptures; video and photographs tell the story of the 5,000-year-old bogwood.
✉ Barley Harbour, Newtowncashel, Co Longford ☎ 043 332 5297
🕐 Mon–Sat 9–6

### Cleo

Clothes made from natural fibres of Irish origin.

✉ 18 Kildare Street, Dublin ☎ 01 676 1421 🕐 Mon–Sat 9–5:30

### Designyard

Features some of the best contemporary Irish craftworkers.

✉ 48–49 Nassau Street, Dublin ☎ 01 474 1011 🕐 Mon–Sat 10–6:30 (to 8pm Thu)

### Kilkenny Design Centre

Superb range of top-quality crafts from all over Ireland.

✉ Castle Yard, Kilkenny, Co Kilkenny ☎ 056 772 2118 🕐 May–Dec Mon–Sat 10–7, Sun 11–7; Jan–Apr Mon–Sat 10–7

### Kilkenny Shop

Made in Ireland is the key here. Large selection of pottery, jewellery, glassware and fashion items. Traditional but with a touch of new creativity.

✉ 6–10 Nassau Street, Dublin ☎ 01 677 7066 🕐 Mon–Wed, Fri 8:30–7, Thu 8:30–8, Sat 8:30–6:30, Sun 11–6

## TRADITIONAL MUSIC

### Celtic Note

Small, specialist Irish music store featuring everything from folk and traditional ballads to rock and contemporary.

✉ 12 Nassau Street, Dublin, Co Dublin ☎ 01 670 4157

### Claddagh Records

A treasure trove of CDs and tapes ranging from Irish dance to traditional and modern.

✉ Cecilia Street, Temple Bar, Dublin ☎ 01 677 0262

## DEPARTMENT STORES

There are large malls at Blackrock (a short walk from the DART Blackrock station), Blanchardstown (north on the N3) and the Liffey Valley Centre (west off the N4, just beyond the M50 interchange).

The Square Shopping Centre at Tallaght, south of Dublin, is a superb modern shopping centre, one of the largest in Ireland, with nearly 150 shops under a huge dome of natural light. Trees and shrubs thrive here, creating an illusion of the outdoors, where it never rains. The centre, open daily, includes supermarkets, restaurants, a crèche (day nursery) and parking for 3,000 cars.

### Arnotts
A major refurbishment has put this store at the forefront of the new-look Northside.

✉ 12 Henry Street, Dublin ☎ 01 805 0400 ⏰ Mon–Sat 10–7 (to 9pm Thu), Sun 12–7

### Brown Thomas
Sophisticated department store, with top-quality goods, including exclusive designer fashions, cosmetics and china. Choice of cafés and a hair salon.

✉ 88–92 Grafton Street, Dublin ☎ 01 605 6666 ⏰ Mon–Sat 9–8 (to 9pm Thu), Sun 11–7

### Clery's
This huge Irish-owned store dominates one side of O'Connell Street. Great for souvenirs as well as general shopping.

✉ O'Connell Street, Dublin ☎ 01 878 6000 ⏰ Mon–Sat 10–7 (to 9pm Thu, 8pm Fri), Sun 12–6

## ENTERTAINMENT

### LIVE MUSIC
### The Button Factory
One of Temple Bar's trendier music venues. It also hosts club nights and a range of cultural events.

✉ Curved Street, Dublin ☎ 01 670 9202

### Johnnie Fox's
Traditional music every day in the famous Hooley sessions.

✉ Glencullen, Co Dublin ☎ 01 295 5647

### O'Shea's Merchant

Huge traditional music and dancing venue down on the quayside on the far side of Temple Bar. Don't be afraid to join in the dancing.

✉ 12 Lower Bridge Street, Dublin ☎ 01 679 3797

### The O2

Vast venue in a former tram depot hosts top superstars.

✉ East Link Bridge, North Wall Quay, Dublin, Co Dublin ☎ 01 836 6777

### Whelans

Famous Dublin venue, hosting traditional Irish, rock, jazz and blues.

✉ 25 Wexford Street, Dublin, Co Dublin ☎ 01 478 0766

## NIGHTCLUBS

### POD

Club scene institution in the vaults of a historic railway station.

✉ 35 Harcourt Street, Dublin ☎ 01 478 0225

### The Twisted Pepper

Hip Middle Abbey Street café/bar venue with club nights taking over Thursday to Saturday.

✉ 54 Middle Abbey Street, Dublin ☎ 01 873 4038; www.bodytonicmusic.com

## THEATRE AND CINEMA

### Abbey Theatre

Internationally famous theatre, renowned for staging classic works by Irish writers such as Brendan Behan and Sean O'Casey.

✉ 26 Abbey Street, Dublin, Co Dublin ☎ 01 878 7222

### Gaiety Theatre

"The Grand Old Lady of South King Street" has been staging performances of all kinds since 1871.

✉ South King Street, Dublin, Co Dublin ☎ 01 677 1717

### Gate Theatre

Drama from modern Irish and international playwrights.

✉ 1 Cavendish Row, Parnell Square, Dublin, Co Dublin ☎ 01 874 4045

# Cork and the South

**A great many visitors to Ireland head straight for this southwestern corner, with its quintessentially Irish look and feel. Here you will find the great fiord-like bays which cut into the rocky west coast, between the magnificent peninsulas of An Daingean (The Dingle), the Iveragh (better known as The Ring of Kerry), the Beara and the smaller, but no less beautiful Sheep's Head and Mizen peninsulas.**

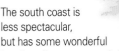

Cork

The south coast is less spectacular, but has some wonderful beaches, fine resorts and charming fishing villages such as Kinsale. Aim to be hungry when you visit here – the village is known as the Gourmet Capital of Ireland.

The southwest is not all coast and scenery. Ireland's second city, Cork, and its third, Limerick, are in this area, while towards the east are the historic city of Waterford, the great Rock of Cashel and the ancient towns and castles along the River Suir.

## CORK

Cork is the Republic's second largest city. At its heart is the wide St Patrick's Street, with lots of lanes leading off that are a delight to explore. Cork is a friendly city, where tradition and modern life blend together easily. It has a vibrant arts and cultural scene and was designated the European Capital of Culture for 2005.

The name Cork comes from the Irish word "Corcaigh", meaning marsh. The older part of the city is on an island in the River Lee. From this island a network of streets branches out, giving a blend of broad malls and narrow lanes, spires, Georgian houses, busy

markets and bridges that make up Cork's most prevalent features. The Lee flows into the deep waters of Cork Harbour, and this harbour brought much of the city's prosperity over the centuries. It also brought the Vikings in AD820 and later the Anglo-Normans. Cork suffered at the hands of William of Orange in 1690 and the "Black and Tans" (a British military force) in the 20th century. Having risen to all these challenges, Cork remains a city of unique character.

✚ 18L

ℹ Grand Parade ☎ 021-425 5100

### Cork Butter Museum

Butter seems an odd subject for a museum, until you discover that Shandon's Butter Exchange was once the largest butter market in the world, attracting customers from distant continents, and that its brand was internationally recognized as a symbol of top quality.

**www**.corkbutter.museum

✉ O'Connell Square, Shandon ☎ 021 430 0600 🕐 Mar–Oct daily 10–1, 2–5 (Jul–Aug 2–6) 👋 Inexpensive 🚌 3 from city centre

### Cork City Gaol

The thought of going to prison, if only for the afternoon, may not appeal, but Cork's former gaol is now a museum that recreates prison life in the 19th century in an entertaining way, and also presents a good social history of the city. The former Governor's House contains the Radio Museum Experience, incorporating a 1927 studio and the RTE Museum Collection.

**www**.corkcitygaol.com

✉ Convent Avenue, Sunday's Well ☎ 021 430 5022 🕐 Mar–Oct daily 9:30–5; Nov–Feb daily 10–4 👋 Moderate 🍴 Coffee shop (€)

## Cork Public Museum

Few city museums have such a lovely setting as this. There are 7.5ha (18.5 acres) of beautiful parkland surrounding the Georgian House, which displays a wide range of collections illustrating the economic and social history of Cork, along with its Civic Regalia.

✉ Fitzgerald Park, Mardyke ☎ 021 427 0679 🕐 Mon–Fri 11–1, 2:15–5, Sat 11–1, 2:15–4, Sun 3–5 (Apr–Sep) ✋ Free

## Crawford Art Gallery

One of Ireland's finest art galleries, the Crawford has a wonderful extension. Above a glass frontage on Half Moon Street, the gallery wall swoops out over the pavement like the hull of a ship, to reflect Cork's maritime heritage. The theme continues inside, in the three curving ceiling sections above the upper galleries, that are flooded with natural light. The lower gallery has a more restrained environment. The next phase of the Crawford Development Plan is to improve the historic original building and the grounds. As well as its permanent collection of works by Irish artists, there are lively temporary exhibitions.

**www.**crawfordartgallery.com

✉ Emmet Place ☎ 021 490 7855 🕐 Mon–Wed, Fri–Sat 10–5, Thu 10–8. Closed 25 Dec–1 Jan ✋ Free 🍽 Crawford Gallery Cafe (€€) 🚌 All city buses 🚆 Cork (10-min walk)

## St Anne's Church

The tall square tower of St Anne's Church, capped by a gilded weathervane in the shape of a salmon, is Cork's best-known landmark. The tower is faced in red and white sandstone – the colours of Cork. Built in 1722, St Anne's is the oldest parish church still in continuous use in Cork. Its famous bells chime each quarter hour. Sunday service is at 10am.

✉ Church Street, Shandon ☎ 021 450 5906 🕐 Easter–Oct daily 9:30–5; Nov–Easter 10–3 ✋ Inexpensive 🚌 3 from city centre

# a walk around Cork

**This walk takes in the main shopping street and the art gallery, before crossing the River Lee to Shandon, then on to the Cork Public Museum in Fitzgerald Park.**

*Walk along Grand Parade away from the statue, then bear right into St Patrick's Street. At the pedestrian crossing, turn left and go along Academy Street to the Crawford Art Gallery (➤ 114).*

This fine municipal gallery has a particularly good collection of local landscapes.

*Continue around the corner and by the Opera House cross the bridge. Turn left, then bear right and follow signs to Shandon for the Butter Museum (▶ 113). Off the square is St Anne's Church (▶ 114).*

This Anglican Communion church is one of Cork's landmarks, with its lofty tower and famous bells.

*Continue, passing the Shandon Arms on the left, and at the end go straight along Chapel Street.*

Opposite the end of Chapel Street is the Cathedral of St Mary and St Ann, with a beautiful, bright interior.

*Turn left along Cathedral Street, then left down Shandon Street to the river. Turn right to walk along the nearside riverbank, then at the end cross a footbridge. Follow the riverside wall then go forward between Mercy Hospital and the University's Lee Maltings. At the end turn right and walk along Dyke Parade until you reach the gates to Fitzgerald Park on the right. The Cork Public Museum is just inside the gates (▶ 114).*

**Distance** About 2.5km (1.5 miles)
**Time** About 3 hours
**Start point** Grand Parade 🚌 All city centre buses
**End point** Fitzgerald Park 🚌 8 to city centre
**Lunch** Bells Bar and Bistro (€€), Crawford Café, Crawford Art Gallery, tel 021 427 4415

# The South

### BANTRY

This lovely little town at the head of
Bantry Bay is a busy fishing port, its
harbour overlooked by a statue of that
intrepid Irish seafarer, St Brendan.
Close by is the entrance to **Bantry
House,** a Georgian mansion filled
with a fine collection of furniture,
Pompeiian mosaics and tapestries. The
Italianate gardens have a wonderful
view over the bay, and delicate plants
thrive in the mild climate.

✚ 16M

**Bantry House**

☎ 027 50047;www.bantryhouse.com

🕓 Mar–Oct daily 10–6 🖐 Expensive 🍴 Tea room (€) 🚌 Cork–Bantry bus
236, 252

### THE BEARA PENINSULA

Less well known than the Ring of Kerry and the Dingle, the Beara
Peninsula is just as beautiful, with its rocky, indented coastline and

offshore islands. The Caha Mountains
and the Slieve Miskish Mountains form
its spine, creating a dramatic inland
landscape, and the Healy Pass, which
zigzags across the Caha range, has
wonderful views (➤ 124).

The **Sub-Tropical Gardens** on
Ilnacullin (Garnish or Garinish Island), in a
sheltered inlet of Bantry Bay, reached by
ferry from Glengarriff, is the Beara's main attraction. It is a
magnificent Italian garden, with a world-famous collection of

plants, which thrive here because of the warming effect of the Gulf Stream.

⊞ 15L

**Sub-Tropical Gardens**

✉ Ilnacullin, off Glengarriff ☎ 027 63040; www.heritageireland.ie
🕐 Jul–Aug Mon–Sat 9:30–6:30, Sun 11–6:30; Apr Mon–Sat 10–6:30, Sun 1–6:30; May, Sep Mon–Sat 10–6:30, Sun 12–6:30; Jun Mon–Sat 10–6:30, Sun 11–6:30; Oct Mon–Sat 10–4; Sun 1–5 ✋ Inexpensive 🚌 236, 252 from Cork 🚢 Glengarriff main street (separate charge for ferry)

## BLARNEY CASTLE

The "gift of the Blarney" is known all over the world and this is where you get it. By leaning backwards over a sheer drop (protected by railings) from the castle battlements and kissing a particular piece of rock, any visitor can go home endowed with a new eloquence. The Blarney Stone is reached by ancient stone spiral staircases through the ruins of the 15th-century castle, which are worth a visit even without its notoriety. The castle is set amid lovely grounds, and is one of Ireland's most visited places.
**www.**blarneycastle.ie

⊞ 17L ✉ Blarney, Co Cork ☎ 021 438 5210 🕐 Jun–Aug Mon–Sat 9–7, Sun 9–5:30; May, Sep Mon–Sat 9–6:30, Sun 9–5:30; Oct–Apr daily 9–dusk ✋ Expensive

## CASHEL

The town tends to be overshadowed by the great Rock of Cashel (▶ 52–53) which dominates the skyline, but as one of Ireland's Heritage Towns, it is well worth a visit in its own right. A good place to start is City Hall, which has historical and folklore displays relating to the town. There is also a **Folk Village,** with a series of 18th- to 20th-century house fronts, shops and memorabilia, and the **Brù Borù Cultural Centre,** which offers folk theatre, evening banquets, exhibitions and traditional music sessions. Added in 2001, 'The Sounds of History' exhibition is located in a

subterranean setting where Ireland's musical heritage is reactivated and enhanced.

www.cashel.ie

✚ 19J 🚌 Dublin–Cork buses 🚉 Thurles 18km (11 miles)

**Folk Village**

✉ Dominic Street ☎ 062 62525 🕐 Daily 10–7:30 (until 6pm in winter) ✋ Moderate

**Brù Borù Cultural Centre**

www.comhaltas.com

☎ 062 61122 🕐 Mid-Jun to mid-Sep daily 9am–11pm, shows Tue–Sat 9pm; mid-Sep to mid-Jun, Mon–Fri 9–1, 2–5, no shows ✋ Exhibition moderate; show expensive 🍴 Self-service restaurant (€). Combined evening meal and show (€€)

## CORCA DHUIBHNE (THE DINGLE PENINSULA)

Best places to see, ➤ 40–41.

## KENMARE

Kenmare's location at the head of Kenmare Bay, surrounded by majestic mountains, earns the town its Irish name "Neidin" or "little nest". Ireland's first planned town was designed by William Petty in 1670. Today, traditional pubs, craft shops and art galleries combine well with first-class hotels, guest houses and award-winning restaurants. The Heritage Centre explains the history of Kenmare using personal audio-tours and exhibitions include exhibits on Kenmare lace and the Nun of Kenmare.

✚ 15L 🍴 P F McCarthy's, Main Street (€€)

ℹ Tourist Information ☎ 064 41233

## THE RING OF KERRY

The road which encircles the Iveragh Peninsula is popularly known as the Ring of Kerry, an exceptionally scenic circular

route of 107km (66 miles) if you start and finish in Killarney. From here you go south through the national park to Kenmare, then along the north shore of the Kenmare estuary, through the lovely resort of Parknasilla. The famous Great Southern Hotel (now the Parknasilla Resort) here has played host to the rich and famous for many years.

Farther along is Caherdaniel. The route heads north from here around Ballinskelligs Bay to Waterville, then on to Cahersiveen, the "capital" of the peninsula and birthplace of the politician Daniel O'Connell. It also has an interesting Heritage Centre. The road then heads eastwards, with Dingle Bay to the north, through Killorglin, a market town famous for its Puck Fair in August, then back to Killarney.

As if the wonderful coast and mountain scenery were not enough, the peninsula is also blessed with a warm Gulf Stream climate.

✚ 14L 🍴 Blind Piper Bar Restaurant (€–€€), Caherdaniel

## KILLARNEY

Killarney is one of the busiest tourist towns in Ireland, not for its own attractions so much as for its surroundings. Although it has many pubs and shops, it is essentially a

base for exploring the beauties of Kerry, and is the traditional starting point for the Ring of Kerry. The Killarney National Park, 10,000ha (24,710 acres) of beautiful mountains, woodland and lakes, is right on the doorstep, and is the setting for Ross Castle (➤ 60) and Muckross House (➤ 46–47).

Jarveys are the drivers of the horse-drawn jaunting cars you will see lined up along the roadside in Killarney. Haggling over the fee is an acceptable part of the deal, but remember that you are not just paying to get from A to B – jarveys are an intrinsic part of the Killarney experience and will usually spin a yarn or two along the way.

✚ 15K

ℹ Tourist Information ☎ 064 663 1663

# a drive around Kerry and Cork

**This drive includes the wonderful wooded mountains of the Killarney National Park, the spectacular Healy Pass and two of Ireland's finest historic houses.**

*From Killarney take the N71, signposted to Muckross, and soon you will reach the Killarney National Park and Muckross House (▶ 46–47).*

Muckross's location amid the mountains and lakes of the national park is unsurpassed.

*Continue on the N71, passing Torc Waterfall, to reach Ladies' View, then after 6km (4 miles), at Molls Gap, bear left, signposted to Kenmare, Glengarriff. At Kenmare drive up the main street and turn right, then leave the town following signs for Glengarriff and Bantry. Cross a river bridge and turn right, signposted Castletown Bearhaven R571. Continue for about 14km (8.5 miles), then follow signs for the Healy Pass.*

This pass across the Caha Mountains has stunning views and a breathtaking summit.

*Over the top of the pass, descend a series of hairpin bends and continue to reach a T-junction. Turn left for Glengarriff or right to lunch in Castletownbere.*

Ilnacullin (Garinish Island), with its beautiful Sub-Tropical Gardens (▶ 118–119), can be reached by ferry from Glengarriff.

*Continue for 5.6km (3.5 miles) to Bantry.*

By the harbour on the Cork road is Bantry House (➤ 118) and the Armada Exhibition.

*Retrace the route to Glengarriff, then take the N71 to Kenmare and Killarney.*

**Distance** 140km (87 miles)
**Time** 6–7 hours depending on attractions visited
**Start/end point** Killarney ✚ 15K
**Lunch** The Copper Kettle (€), The Square, Castletownbere, tel 027 71792, open Mon–Sat

## KINSALE

Kinsale is a delightful little town 29km (18 miles) from Cork City. It offers visitors such things as sailing, scenery, history and good food. The annual Gourmet Festival in October and a Good Food Circle work to maintain the town's famously high culinary standards. Historically, Kinsale is remembered for the 1601 battle when a Spanish fleet came to aid Hugh O'Neill's struggle against the English. The Irish/Spanish force was defeated, thus marking the decline of the old Gaelic order, with the "Flight of the Earls" to Europe. The late 17th-century Charles Fort at Summercove is open to visitors, while James Fort is in ruins but is still worth a visit for the grand views of the town and harbour. It was off this coast that the *Lusitania* was sunk by a German submarine in 1915, with the loss of 1,500 lives. Places of interest to visit in Kinsale include the Courthouse, *c*1600, which now houses a regional museum

✚ 17M 🍴 Fishy Fishy (€€, ➤ 132) ℹ️ Tourist Information ☎ 021 477 2234

### LIMERICK

The Republic's third largest city, Limerick is a cultural centre, well endowed with theatres, art galleries and museums – notably the **Hunt Museum.** Located in the elegant 18th-century Custom House, the gallery has one of the greatest private collections of art and antiquities in the country.

The River Shannon flows through the city, overlooked by **King John's Castle** and crossed by many fine bridges. The oldest part of the city is on King's Island, first settled by the Vikings, and it is here that the most important historical sites are found, including the castle and the 12th-century Protestant cathedral.

The city's architecture is jealously guarded by the Limerick Civic Trust. The best old street is The Crescent, while examples of modern architecture are the Civic Centre and City Hall on Merchant's Quay.

✚ 17J

**Hunt Museum**

✉ Custom House, Rutland Street ☎ 061 312833; www.huntmuseum.com
🕐 Mon–Sat 10–5, Sun 2–5 ✋ Moderate (free Sun) 🍴 Restaurant (€€)
🚌 All city centre buses

**King John's Castle**

✚ Nicholas Street, King's Island ☎ 061 360788 🕐 Apr–Oct daily 10–5:30; Nov–Mar daily 10:30–4:30 ✋ Moderate


### MUCKROSS HOUSE

Best places to see, ➤ 46–47.


### THE ROCK OF CASHEL

Best places to see, ➤ 52–53.

## WATERFORD

Waterford grew from an ancient Viking settlement into the foremost port in Ireland, and its quays are still busy with international trade; the famous **Waterford Crystal Visitor Centre** reflects this. The city preserves an atmosphere of the past, and the mixture of Celt, Viking, Norman, English, Huguenot and Flemish gives a European flavour which is reflected on the seafront and in its narrow lanes. One of the oldest buildings is Reginald's Tower, built by the Vikings in 1003, which now houses the city museum. The Church of Ireland cathedral is regarded as the finest 18th-century ecclesiastical building in Ireland, and the Catholic cathedral has superb carving and stained glass.

✚ 20K

### Waterford Crystal Visitor Centre

✉ The Mall ☎ 051 332500; www.waterfordvisitorcentre.com 🕐 Visitor centre and shop: Jun–Sep Mon–Sat 9–6, Sun 10:3-–6; Oct–May daily 9–5. Tours: Jun–Sep Mon–Sat 9–4:15, Sun 10:30–4:15; Oct–May Mon–Fri 9–3:15
🖐 Moderate 🍴 Restaurant (€–€€) 🚌 Waterford–Ballybeg

## HOTELS

### ADARE, CO LIMERICK
**Adare Manor (€€€)**
An opulent hotel in a Gothic mansion, surrounded by parkland beside the River Maigue. Includes a championship golf course and other leisure facilities.
✉ On Limerick to Tralee route ☎ 061 605200; www.adaremanor.com

### CLONAKILTY, CO CORK
**Inchydoney Island Lodge & Spa (€€€)**
Modern coastal hotel in a blue-flag beach setting. Home to Ireland's only thalassotherapy (seawater) spa.
✉ Clonakilty, West Cork ☎ 023 883 3143; www.inchydoneyisland.com

### CORK, CO CORK
**Clarion Hotel (€€–€€€)**
With its prominent quayside street corner location, you couldn't ask for a better view over Cork City and down the River Lee into Cork Harbour. The friendly staff render this a cut above other more "corporate" hotels.
✉ Lapps Quay ☎ 021 422 4900; www.clarionhotelcorkcity.com

**Hotel Isaacs (€€)**
One of Cork's finest hotels, with good accommodation and the celebrated Greenes Restaurant.
✉ 48 MacCurtain Street ☎ 021 450 0011; www.isaacs.ie

### KENMARE, CO KERRY
**Park Hotel (€€€)**
Country-house hotel overlooking Kenmare Bay and home to the deluxe spa "Samas" Each bedroom is individually decorated with antiques and *objets d'art*.
✉ On the R569 ☎ 064 664 1200; www.parkkenmare.com ⏱ Closed Jan–Mar

**Sallyport House (€€)**
This 1932, antique-filled family home has been enlarged into a

delightful bed-and-breakfast, with lovely grounds including an orchard.

✉ Glengariff Road ☎ 064 664 2066; www.sallyporthouse.com

## KILLARNEY, CO KERRY
### Aghadoe Heights (€€€)

In a superb setting high above the Killarney Lakes, this hotel offers luxury and hospitality and an excellent restaurant.

✉ 5km (3 miles) north of Killarney, off the N22 Tralee road ☎ 064 663 1766; www.aghadoeheights.com ⏰ Closed Jan–Mar

## LIMERICK, CO LIMERICK
### No 1 Pery Square (€€–€€€)

Overlooking the People's Park in Limerick's Georgian quarter, this delightful hotel has a number of rooms decorated in period style to match the Georgian theme.

✉ 1 Pery Square ☎ 061 402402; www.oneperysquare.com

## WATERFORD, CO WATERFORD
### The Tower Hotel (€€)

In the heart of the city overlooking the waterfront and Reginald's Tower, this supremely convenient, family-friendly hotel is a good base for touring the area.

✉ The Mall ☎ 051 870129; www.towerhotelwaterford.com

# RESTAURANTS

## BALLINGARRY, CO LIMERICK
### The Mustard Seed (€€€)

A pleasant drive through the Limerick countryside on quiet lanes leads to this first-class restaurant in a stylish country house. Also offers B&B.

✉ Echo Lodge ☎ 069 68508; www.mustardseed.ie ⏰ Daily dinner

## BALTIMORE, CO CORK
### Chez Youen (€€–€€€)

Among the best fish restaurants in Ireland.

✉ The Waterfront Hotel, The Square ☎ 028 20136; www.waterfronthotel.ie

✪ Summer Mon–Sat lunch, dinner, Sun lunch; winter Thu–Sat lunch, dinner, Sun lunch

## BANTRY, CO CORK
### O'Connor's Seafood Restaurant (€–€€)
Fresh local fish and shellfish are the specialities here.
✉ The Square ☎ 027 50221; www.oconnorseafood.com ✪ Sun–Fri lunch, dinner, Sat dinner

## CLOGHROE, CO CORK
### Blairs Inn (€–€€)
In a secluded riverside setting near Blarney. Good Irish cuisine, including fish, duck, steaks and game, all from local sources. Traditional music on Mondays (summer only).
✉ Cloghroe, Blarney ☎ 021 438 1470; www.blairsinn.ie ✪ Daily 12:30–9

## CORK, CO CORK
### Farmgate Café (€–€€)
See page 59.

### Hayfield Manor (€€–€€€)
Flickering candles and soft lighting set the tone for this high-end restaurant near the university. Expect modern Irish cuisine using fine local produce and a good wine list.
✉ Perrott Avenue, College Road ☎ 021 484 5900; www.hayfieldmanor.ie
✪ Daily lunch dinner, and Sun afternoon tea

## DINGLE, CO KERRY
### The Chart House (€€)
Excellent cuisine in this popular harbourside restaurant.
✉ The Mall ☎ 066 915 2255 ✪ Wed–Mon 6:30–10; closed 6 Jan–13 Feb

### Lord Baker's (€–€€)
Fish, game and succulent steaks are the speciality of this excellent restaurant.
✉ Main Street ☎ 066 915 1277; www.lordbakers.ie ✪ Fri–Wed 12:30–2, 6–10

## KENMARE, CO KERRY
### Packie's (€€)
Stylish but unpretentious restaurant with creative cooking;
intensely flavoured Irish-Mediterranean food.
✉ Henry Street ☎ 064 41508 🕔 Mon–Sat 6–10; closed mid-Jan to Feb

### Prego (€–€€)
Good atmosphere and tasty Italian food using local produce in this
well-priced family restaurant.
✉ Henry Street ☎ 064 42350 🕔 Daily 9am–10:30pm

## KILLARNEY, CO KERRY
### Chapter 40 (€€)
A contemporary restaurant picking flavours from all over the world.
The tapas are popular, as is the chef's eclectic Tasting Plate.
✉ 40 New Street ☎ 064 667 1833; www.chapter40.ie 🕔 Tue–Sat 5–10

### Foley's Seafood and Steak Restaurant (€€–€€€)
The name says it all, and the restaurant is famous for it.
✉ 23 High Street ☎ 064 31217 🕔 Daily 5–10:30

## KINSALE, CO CORK
### Fishy Fishy (€€)
Fresh fish, shellfish, salads and desserts feature in this popular
seafood speciality eatery.
✉ Market Place ☎ 021 477 4453 🕔 Daily 10–4

### Man Friday (€€–€€€)
One of Kinsale's longest-established restaurants, with an excellent
reputation for its modern Irish and international cuisine.
✉ Scilly ☎ 021 477 2260 🕔 Mon–Sat 6:30–10:15

## LIMERICK, CO LIMERICK
### The Locke Bar (€–€€)
Facing the Abbey River, this ancient pub/restaurant makes a good
stopping point between the Hunt Museum and St John's Castle.
✉ 3 Georges Quay ☎ 061 413733; www.lockebar.com 🕔 Daily lunch, dinner

### Mortell's (€)

Fish and chips in Limerick can only mean Mortell's. It's a simple café, but it serves only the best local catch.

✉ 49 Roches Street ☎ 061 415457 🕐 Mon–Sat 8–5:30

### NEW ROSS, CO WATERFORD
#### The Galley Cruising Restaurant (€€€)

Cruising restaurants ply the waters of the rivers Barrow and Nore from New Ross and Waterford, offering a wonderfully relaxing way to eat and enjoy the scenery at the same time. Lunch, afternoon tea and dinner cruises are all available. Reservations essential.

✉ The Quay, New Ross ☎ 051 421723; www.rivercruises.ie 🕐 Apr–Oct

### WATERFORD, CO WATERFORD
#### Fitzpatrick's Manor Lodge (€€–€€€)

A beautifully restored house is home to this Gallic-flavoured fine restaurant, where seafood is the speciality.

✉ Cork Road ☎ 051 378851 🕐 Tue–Fri, Sun 12–9:30, Sat 5–9:30

## SHOPPING

### ANTIQUES
#### Frameworks

Irish prints, pictures and maps are the speciality at this Kerry antiquarian shop. There is also an interesting range of 18th- and 19th-century furniture.

✉ 37 New Street, Killarney, Co Kerry ☎ 086 239 0033; www.frameworks.ie

#### George Stackpole

Antiques and books, bought and sold.

✉ Main Street, Adare, Co Limerick ☎ 061 396409

### CRAFTS
#### Black Abbey Crafts

Good selection of quality Irish crafts, including ceramics, slate, iron and glass items.

✉ Adare Heritage Centre, Co Limerick ☎ 061 396021 🕐 Daily 9–6

### Blarney Woollen Mills

First established in 1750, the company now offers woven rugs and Aran sweaters, plus crystal, china and gifts.

✉ Blarney, Co Cork ☎ 021 451 6111; www.blarney.ie 🕐 Mon–Sat 9:30–6, Sun 10–6

### Louis Mulcahy Pottery

This renowned pottery sells quality hand-painted lampshades, sculpted masks, dinner services and much more.

✉ Clogher Head, West Dingle, Co Kerry ☎ 066 915 6229; www.louismulcahy.com 🕐 Jun–Aug Mon–Fri 9–7, Sat–Sun 10–7; Easter–May, Sep–Oct Mon–Fri 9–6, Sat–Sun 10–6; Nov–Easter Mon–Fri 9–5:30, Sat 10–5:30, Sun 11–5:30

## MARKETS
### The English Market

Daily covered market with array of food stalls.

✉ Princes Street/St Patrick's Street/Grand Parade, Cork, Co Cork

### Milk Market

Retail outlets open all week; arts and crafts market on Friday; traditional market Saturday morning.

✉ Corn Market Row, Limerick, Co Limerick

## SHOPPING CENTRES
### Arthur's Quay Shopping Centre

Very attractive collection of over 30 stores in a prime city-centre location; restaurants, day nursery, play area and plenty of parking.

✉ Limerick, Co Limerick ☎ www.arthursquay-shopping.com

### Killarney Outlet Centre

More than 20 shops, including a Nike factory store.

✉ Fair Hill, Killarney ☎ www.killarneyoutletcentre.com

### Merchant's Quay Shopping Centre

Big high street brands under one roof.

✉ 1 St. Patrick's Street, Cork, Co Cork ☎ www.merchantsquaycork.com

## TRADITIONAL MUSIC

### The Soundz of Music

Good range of CDs including traditional Irish music and instruments.

✉ Henry Street, Kenmare, Co Kerry ☎ 064 644 2268

### Variety Sounds

A wide range of guitars, *bodhráns*, whistles and other traditional Irish and folk instruments, as well as CDs and books.

✉ 7 College Street, Killarney, Co Kerry ☎ 064 663 5755

## ENTERTAINMENT

## LIVE MUSIC

### An Droichead Beag

A traditional music venue at the heart of Dingle town. Popular with tourists and locals alike.

✉ Main Street, Dingle, Co Kerry ☎ 066 915 1723

### An Spailpín Fánach

Opposite the Murphy's brewery building, this labyrinthine pub is host to traditional sessions by students from the local music college. The name means "the wandering labourer".

✉ 28 South Main Street, Cork, Co Cork ☎ 021 427 7949

### Crane Lane Theatre

Inspired by the music of Tom Waits, the Crane Lane Theatre is part bar, part late night venue. The music tends to be on the jazzy/bluesy side. Entry is often free for gigs.

✉ Phoenix Street, Cork, Co Cork ☎ 021 427 8487; www.cranelanetheatre.com

### Crowley's

If it's tradition you are seeking you'll find it here in the heart of Kenmare. Impromptu Irish music sessions take place regularly.

✉ Henry Street, Kenmare, Co Kerry ☎ 064 664 1472

### De Barra's Pub

Famous landmark pub featuring live folk and traditional music.

✉ Pearse Street, Clonakilty, Co Cork ☎ 023 883 3381; www.debarra.ie

## INEC

Now established as a major venue on the arena circuit, this Killarney convention centre has hosted artists as diverse as Kris Kristofferson, Snow Patrol and the Wiggles.

✉ Muckross Road, Killarney, Co Kerry ☎ 064 667 1555; www.inec.ie

## NIGHTCLUB
### The Corner House

Dark yet spacious northside music haven with artwork and music reflecting an eclectic Cork scene.

✉ 7 Coburg Street, Cork, Co Cork ☎ 021 450 0655

## THEATRE
### Belltable Arts Centre

A reputable venue for theatre, concerts, dance, mime and poetry readings.

✉ 69 O'Connell Street, Limedrick, Co Limerick ☎ 061 319866; www.belltable.ie

### Cork Opera House

The only purpose-built opera house in Ireland is also a venue for musicals, drama and comedy.

✉ Emmet Place, Cork, Co Cork ☎ 021 427 0022; www.corkoperahouse.ie

### Siamsa Tire – The National Folk Theatre of Ireland

Keeping the national traditions alive – Siamsa (pronounced shee-am-sah) is a Gaelic word describing the type of impromptu entertainment country folk would indulge in.

✉ Town Park, Tralee, Co Kerry ☎ 066 712 3055; www.siamsatire.com

### Theatre Royal

Hosts the Opera Festival and The Waterford Show.

✉ The Mall, Waterford, Co Waterford ☎ 051 874402; www.theatreroyal.ie

### Triskel Arts Centre

Drama, readings, children's theatre and music.

✉ Tobin Street, Cork, Co Cork ☎ 021 427 2022

# Galway and the West

**The wild beauty of the west is underlaid with the hostility of a landscape that does its best to defy cultivation. Fields are the size of pocket handkerchiefs, and the drystone walls that enclose them have by no means used up all of the land's loose rocks.**

Galway

Vast empty areas of blanket bog have pockets of wetness that expand into a network of lakes and rivers beneath the mountains of Connemara and Joyce's Country. The great Loughs – Conn, Mask and Corrib – lie between Sligo and Galway bays. Farther east the River Shannon forms the backbone of a watery highway. In Clare, The Burren is a moonscape of bare limestone, where plants cling on to the sparse soil, and the western boundary of all this is a jagged and spectacular coastline.

## GALWAY

Galway, the historic capital of Connaught, is Ireland's fourth largest city, with a delightful blend of ancient and modern. It has at its heart a maze of narrow streets, lined with a mixture of modern shopfronts, traditional-style painted facades, old pubs and restaurants. A relaxed west-coast atmosphere prevails, enlivened by an energetic student population.

Situated in the northeast corner of Galway Bay, where the River Corrib pours into the sea, Galway was built on international trade and sea fishing, and its oldest parts cluster around the harbour and riverside quays. On the east bank is the Spanish Arch, built to protect cargoes of wine and brandy from Iberia. Behind the quay is a network of narrow streets, leading off from the main thoroughfare. A modern shopping mall, incorporating part of the medieval city wall, is hidden away behind old facades. On the far side of the river is The Claddagh, once a close-knit, Gaelic-speaking fishing community and now remembered in the continuing tradition of the Claddagh ring, with two hands holding a crowned heart.

Apart from its own attractions, Galway is a good base for exploring the surrounding areas – Connemara, Lough Corrib, the Aran Islands and the Burren.

Salthill is Galway's seaside resort suburb, to the west, offering a long sandy beach and amusements.

**www**.discoverireland.ie

➕ 17G

ℹ️ Aras Failte, Forster Street ☎ 091 537700

### Cathedral of Our Lady Assumed into Heaven and St Nicholas

Overlooking the River Corrib near the Salmon Weir Bridge, this splendid modern Roman Catholic

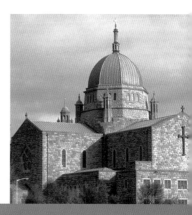

cathedral opened in 1965 and looked so grand that the locals dubbed it the "Taj Michael", after the then Bishop of Galway, Michael (pronounced Mee-hawl) Brown. Built on the site of the former county gaol (jail), it's topped by a great copper dome, and the interior is plain but impressive, with floors of Connemara marble, rough-hewn limestone walls and superb stained glass. It was designed by John J Robinson and replaced the old cathedral on Abbeygate Street, which has been converted into shops.
**www.**galwaycathedral.ie

✉ University and Gaol roads ☎ 091 563577 🕓 Daily 8:30–6:30 💵 Free (donations welcome)

### Nora Barnacle House Museum

Built around the end of the 19th century, this tiny cottage now houses one of the smallest museums in Ireland. It was formerly the home of the eponymous Nora Barnacle, companion, wife and lifelong inspiration of the writer James Joyce. He is said to have based the character of Molly Bloom in his novel *Ulysses* on her. Even without the collections of memorabilia, it is impossible to ignore the romantic associations.

✉ 8 Bowling Green ☎ 091 564743 🕓 Mid-May to mid-Sep Mon–Sat 10–5 💵 Inexpensive

### St Nicholas's Church

St Nicholas's Church is the largest medieval parish church in Ireland still in constant use. It was built around 1320 by the Lynch family and consecrated to the patron saint of sailors. Christopher Columbus worshipped here in 1477, and was no doubt inspired by tales of St Brendan the Navigator, an Irish monk who sailed to America in the 6th century. Outside the church, on the site of the former college, there is a colourful weekly Saturday market. St Nicholas's hosts concerts throughout the year.
**www.**stnicholas.ie

✉ Church Lane 🕓 Daily 11–5; check for services

# a walk around Galway

*From Eyre Square, the heart of the city, walk along William Street, Shop Street and High Street. At the cobbled crossroads walk straight on along Quay Street.*

On the corner is Thomas Dillon's Claddagh Gold, a little jeweller's shop with a Claddagh Ring Museum in the back room. At the end is the famous Spanish Arch, where Iberian traders would land their cargoes, behind which is the new Galway City Museum.

*Take the riverside path that leads off between the bridge and Jury's Hotel. Cross the next road and continue alongside the river on your left, and a millstream on your right. At the end of the path, cross a footbridge over the canal, then turn left and walk to the Salmon Weir Bridge. Cross the bridge*

*and the Cathedral of Our Lady Assumed into Heaven
and St Nicholas is immediately ahead.*

The cathedral, completed in 1965, is topped by a great
copper dome. The interior is light, spacious and, though
plain, is still very impressive.

*Recross the bridge and turn right down Newtown Smith,
passing the footbridge crossed earlier. Walk straight on,
turn right at the crossroads, then at the end bear left.
About halfway along on the right is the Nora Barnacle
House Museum.*

This tiny cottage is where the writer James Joyce courted
his future wife. Mementoes of the couple are on display.

*At the end, opposite St Nicholas's Church, turn left
into Market Street, then right into Upper Abbeygate
Street.*

The building at the end, on the
right, is Lynch's Castle, now
the Allied Irish Bank.

*Turn left into William Street
and return to Eyre Square.*

**Distance** About 2km (1.2 miles)
**Time** 2–3 hours
**Start/end point** Eyre Square
🚌 All city-centre buses
**Lunch** McDonagh's Seafood House
(€–€€€), 22 Quay Street, tel 091
565001. Restaurant: Mon–Sat
5–10pm. Fish and chip bar: Mon–Sat
12–11, Sun 4–10

## The West

### BUNRATTY CASTLE AND FOLK PARK

Bunratty, 14.5km (9 miles) northeast of Limerick, is Ireland's most complete medieval castle, thanks to the restoration work carried out in 1960 when it was purchased by Bord Failte and Lord Gort. Following the restoration, Lord Gort installed his collections of furniture, objets d'art, paintings and tapestries, all of which predate 1650. The castle is famous for its medieval banquets, with historic costume and traditional food and entertainment.

In the castle grounds, Irish village life at the end of the 19th century has been recreated, with reconstructed urban and rural dwellings, farmhouses, a watermill, forge and village street, complete with shops and a pub – all brought to life by

knowledgeable costumed guides. The Regency walled garden and agricultural museum are added attractions.

**www.**shannonheritage.com

⊞ 17J ✉ N18 Bunratty ☎ 061 360788 ⏰ Daily 9–5:30. Last admission 45 mins before closing 👋 Expensive 🍴 Tea room (€); lunches in barn May–Oct (€); Mac's Pub (€€) 🚌 From Limerick, Ennis, Galway 🚆 Limerick, Ennis

## THE BURREN AND AILLWEE CAVE

The Burren National Park preserves a remarkable landscape. It is a vast plateau of limestone hills which were scraped free of their soil by retreating glaciers 15,000 years ago, then eroded by rain and Atlantic mists. The tiny amounts of soil that gather in the rock fissures support both Alpine and Mediterranean plant life, and early summer is the main flowering season. **The Burren Centre** at Kilfenora provides an overview of the area and

its unique landscape. **Aillwee Cave,** south of Ballyvaughan, has fossil formations and water figures. The Burren is best appreciated on foot, and the waymarked 42km (26-mile) Burren Way, from Ballyvaughan to Liscannor, can be undertaken in short sections.

⊞ 17H (The Burren); 16G (Aillwee Cave)

### Burren Centre

**www.**theburrencentre.ie

✉ Kilfenora ☎ 065 708 8030 ⏰ Jun–Aug daily.9:30–5:30; mid-Mar to May, Sep–Oct 10–5 👋 Moderate

### Aillwee Cave

✉ Ballyvaughan ☎ 065 707 7036 ⏰ Tours only: daily from 10am, last tour 5 (Jul and Aug 6); Dec by appointment only 👋 Expensive

## CASTLEBAR

Castlebar is the county town of Co Mayo. Its most notable attraction is the **Museum of Country Life.** Housed in a renovated 18th-century building, along with purpose-built extensions and grounds, this is the first branch of the National Museum to be located outside Dublin. Displays utilizing 50,000 items reflect the lives of Ireland's people and their trades, illustrating the social history of Ireland over the past 200 years.

✚ 4E

**Museum of Country Life**

✉ Turlough Park House ☎ 094 903 1773; www.museum.ie
🕐 Tue–Sat 10–5, Sun 2–5 🍽 Restaurant

## CLIFFS OF MOHER

These towering cliffs rise sheer out of the turbulent Atlantic to a height of nearly 213m (700ft) and stretch for 8km (5 miles) along the Clare coast north of Hag's Head. Majestic in calm weather, the cliffs are most dramatic (and dangerous) when stormy seas crash into their base, hurling pebbles high up into the air. Horizontal layers of flagstones have been exposed by coastal erosion, making ideal perches for the sea birds, including puffins, which abound here. At the highest point of the cliffs, **O'Brien's Tower** was constructed in the early 19th century as a lookout point for the first tourists, and gives views of the Clare coastline, the Oileáin Árann (Aran Islands) and mountains as far apart as Kerry and Connemara. The controversial Atlantic Edge visitor centre opened behind the cliffs in 2007.

✚ 16H

**O'Brien's Tower and Visitor Centre**

✉ Near Liscannor ☎ 065 708 6141 🕐 Tower: daily 10–5. Visitor Centre: Jul–Aug daily 9–9:30; Jun 9–7:30; May, Sep 9–7; Apr 9–6:30; Mar, Oct 9–6; Nov–Feb 9:15–5 💷 Inexpensive; nearby parking €8 per car 🍽 Restaurant (€–€€) 🚍 From Lahinch and other nearby towns

## CLONMACNOISE

Best places to see, ➤ 38–39.

## CONNEMARA

To the northwest of Galway City is Connemara, home to some of the most dramatic scenery in Ireland. Much of its convoluted

coastline, with masses of tiny islands and some excellent beaches, can be followed by road and the views are spectacular. Inland, in southern Connemara, are thousands of lakes amid the bogland. Farther north, and hardly ever out of sight, are the brooding ranges of the Twelve Pins and the Maumturk Mountains, with wonderful hiking opportunities. Connemara marble is quarried at Recess, and there is a factory shop and showroom at Connemara Marble Industries in Moycullen. The Connemara National Park protects about 2,000ha (4,940 acres) of the mountains, bogs, heaths and grasslands. There's a good **visitor centre** in Letterfrack and a herd of Connemara ponies.

**www.**connemaranationalpark.ie

✚ 3F

**National Park Visitor Centre**

✉ Letterfrack ☎ 095 41054 🕐 Daily 9–5:30
💷 Inexpensive 🍴 Tea rooms (€) ❓ Guided walks
Jun–Aug. Talks and special events for children

## DONEGAL

Donegal tweed has made the name of this northwest corner of
Ireland familiar around the world. In the old province of Ulster, it
was one of the three counties that was placed in the Irish Free
State after partition in 1922 (Monaghan and Cavan were the other
two). It's a rugged county with high sea cliffs facing the Atlantic,
especially at Slieve League, west of Killybegs, where they rise to
an impressive 600m (1,970ft). That's almost three times higher
than the more famous Cliffs of Moher in Clare (▶ 144).

Donegal is a modest little town, but it has the remains of two
castles and two abbeys, and is attractively set at the head of
Donegal Bay. **Donegal Castle**, on the bank of the River Eske in the
town centre, was built in 1505 for Red Hugh O'Donnell and was
considerably enlarged in the 17th century for Sir Basil Brooke. The
Brooke family also owned Lough Eske Castle, a Jacobean-style
house damaged by fire in 1939. South of the town are the ruins of
Donegal Abbey. The Annals of the Four Masters was written here
in the 17th century, charting the history of Ireland up until 1616.
This important chronicle is now in the National Library in Dublin.

Probably Ireland's most remote national park, **Glenveagh** is also
its second oldest. The former shooting estate of the Adair family
was given to the nation in 1983 by its American owner, Henry P
McIlhenny. The park contains Ireland's largest herd of red deer and,
since 2000, has been the country's only haunt of the golden eagle.
The solitude of the countryside here is particularly poignant as
John Adair evicted 244 of his tenants in the 19th century to
improve the view from the castle. Adair made his money in land
speculation in America before returning to Ireland determined to
establish a country estate greater than that of Queen Victoria in
Balmoral, Scotland. You can see his Scots baronial-style castle,
with its opulent furnishings, on a guided tour.

Anvil-shaped **Inishowen**. between Lough Foyle in the east and
Lough Swilly in the west, is Ireland's largest peninsula. It's a land
of hills and bogs, with most settlement around the coast. Here

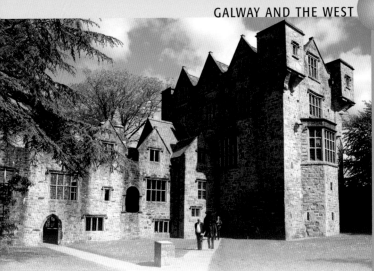

you'll find some exceptional beaches, such as the 5km (3-mile) White Strand at Buncrana and more remote Tullagh Strand near Clonmany. The northern tip of Inishowen is Malin Head, Ireland's most northerly point, facing the wild North Atlantic. Just outside Londonderry, the Grianan of Aileach is a spectacular hillfort, once the seat of the local O'Neill kings of Ulster. The site, which dates back to the Neolithic Age, was restored in the 19th century and commands dramatic views, not just across Donegal, but over Tyrone and Londonderry in Northern Ireland.

**www**.heritageireland.ie

### Donegal Castle

➕ 6C ✉ Tinchonaill Street, Donegal ☎ 074 972 2405 🌐 Easter to mid-Sep daily 10–6; mid-Sep to Easter Thu–Mon 9:30–4:30 ✋ Inexpensive

### Glenveagh National Park

**www**.glenveaghnationalpark.ie

➕ 6B ✉ Glenveagh, Churchill, Letterkenny, Co Donegal ☎ 074 913 7090
🌐 Mar–Oct daily 10–6; Nov–Feb 9–5. Last admission 1 hour before closing
✋ Free. Castle: moderate 🍴 Restaurant (€–€€) Easter, Jun–Sep

### Inishowen Peninsula

**www**.glenveaghnationalpark.ie

➕ 8A ℹ Railway Road, Buncrana ☎ 074 936 2600 🚌 Lough Swilly buses from Londonderry to Buncrana, Clonmany and Greencastle

## KNAPPOGUE CASTLE

Built in the mid-15th century for the MacNamara family, Knappogue underwent many changes over the course of the next five centuries. It was extended and adapted and used as government offices for a while, before falling into a ruinous state. In the 1960s it was acquired by Mark Edwin Andrews, then Assistant Secretary to the US Navy. He and his wife set about the task of restructuring the castle into an authentic setting for the medieval banquets which continue to be popular. They include dinner and a pageant, with stories of the history of the women of Ireland – real and legendary. The castle was acquired by the Shannon Development Company in 1996.

➕ 17H ✉ Kilmurry, near Quin ☎ 061 360788 ⏰ May–Sep daily 10–5. Last admission 4:15 ✋ Moderate ❓ Medieval banquets on demand

## KYLEMORE ABBEY

Kylemore Abbey's greatest attraction is its location. Nestled at the base of Duchruach Mountain, and on the north shores of Lough Pollacapul in the heart of the Connemara Mountains, it is regarded as one of Ireland's most romantic buildings. Lying in a rhododendron-filled hollow, this neo-Gothic estate castle was constructed for British shipping magnate and Irish politican Mitchell Henry. Since 1920 it has been a convent of the Irish Benedictine nuns, and a girls' boarding school now occupies the building. It offers the warmth and hospitality of its peaceful setting to visitors from all over the world. The restaurant has the best of home cooking and a range of the abbey's distinctive pottery can be seen in the studio. Within the grounds there is a Gothic chapel, which has a Connemara marble interior. Nearby is a *taghallai*, a pre-Christian tomb. The 2.5ha (6-acre) restored Victorian walled garden is well worth a visit, as is the visitor centre.

**www.**kylemoreabbey.com

 2F 🖂 Connemara ☎ 095-41146 🕒 Mid-Mar to Oct daily 9:30–5:30; Nov to mid-Mar 10–4:30 ✋ Expensive 🍴 Restaurant (€–€€)

### OILEÁIN ÁRANN (ARAN ISLANDS)

Best places to see, ➤ 50–51.

### THE SHANNON

Ireland's longest river, the Shannon rises in a humble pool (called the Shannon Pot) in Co Cavan, then gathers strength as it flows through a series of lakes before it meets the Atlantic beyond Limerick. Monasteries and castles were built along the river, and river crossings were points where towns grew and prospered. Places such as Carrick-on-Shannon and Athlone are bases for leisure cruiser holidays for which this mighty river is so popular.

🔲 16J

ℹ️ Shannon Development ☎ 061 361555

## SLIGO

Sligo is a lively and attractive town with splendid old shop-fronts and traditional music pubs. It is also a significant cultural centre and has a fine range of art galleries and museums, as well as the various festivals which take place throughout the year.

Over 1,000 years of history have shaped the town, but it is it's literary heritage that attracts many of its visitors. This is Yeats country, and the subject of one of his best-known poems is just outside the town – the Isle of Inisfree in Lough Gill (riverboat trips to the lough depart from Sligo's Doorly Park). Sligo also has two fine cathedrals and Sligo Abbey, a Dominican friary founded in 1252.

✠ 5D

ℹ Temple Street ☎ 071 916 1201

## WESTPORT

Set on Clew Bay, Westport is one of the liveliest and most charming towns in the west of Ireland, with broad Georgian streets and a leafy riverside avenue at its heart. Nearby **Westport House** dates from the 1730s and is the only stately home open to the public in Sligo. It is beautifully furnished and has some superb Waterford crystal, silver and paintings. The dungeons are from an earlier

building, reputedly a castle belonging to Grace O'Malley, the 16th-century pirate queen, and the grounds contain the Pirate Adventure Park.

➕ 3E

**Westport House**

✉ The Quay, Westport ☎ 098 25430/27766; www.westporthouse.ie

🕐 Mid-Mar to Sep daily 10–5 (later in high season); Mar, Oct Sat–Sun 10–4

✋ Expensive 🍴 Café Jun, Aug only (€)

## YEATS TOWER, THOOR BALLYLEE

In 1917 the poet William Butler Yeats bought this derelict 16th-century tower house and renovated it. For the next 12 years he and his family spent their summers here and it was in these peaceful surroundings that he wrote most of his works. His life-long friend and patron, Lady Gregory, lived nearby, and together they were the inspiration behind the Irish Literary Revival and the founding of the Abbey Theatre in Dublin (➤ 110). In the 1960s Thoor Ballylee was again restored, to show how it looked when Yeats was here.

➕ 17G ✉ Gort ☎ 091 631436 (off season 091-537700) 🕐 May–Sep Mon–Sat 9:30–5 ✋ Moderate ❓ Audio-visual presentation and displays of first editions. Bookshop, craft centre, picnic area

## HOTELS

### BALLYVAUGHAN, CO CLARE
#### Drumcreehy House (€)
Just 1.5km (1 mile) north of the village and across the road from the sea, this bed-and-breakfast has character and style, with German and Irish antiques everywhere.

✉ Ballyvaughan ☎ 065 707 7377; www.drumcreehyhouse.com

### BUNRATTY, CO CLARE
#### Bunratty Woods Country House (€–€€)
Situated in the grounds of Bunratty Castle, this guest house contains many interesting antiques and has mountain views.

✉ Low Road ☎ 061 369689 ☻ Closed 7 Nov–early Mar

### CASHEL, CO GALWAY
#### Cashel House (€€€)
Gracious country-house hotel in superb gardens overlooking Cashel Bay.

✉ Off the N59, 1.5km (1 mile) west of Recess ☎ 095 31001; www.cashel-house-hotel.com ☻ Closed early Jan–early Feb

### CASTLEREA, CO ROSCOMMON
#### Clonalis House (€€€)
Clonalis House is the home of the O'Conors of Connacht, descendants of the Kings of Connacht and the last High King of Ireland. Guests here can browse through old family manuscripts and see the harp which belonged to the great Turlough O'Carolan.

✉ On the west side of Castlerea on the N60 ☎ 949 620014; www.clonalis.com ☻ Closed Oct–Mar

### CLIFDEN, CO GALWAY
#### The Quay House (€€)
Overlooking the harbour, about 500m (550yds) from the town centre, this comfortable hideaway offers individually designed rooms and one of the best breakfasts in Connemara.

✉ Beach Road, Clifden ☎ 095 21369; www.thequayhouse.com ☻ Closed Nov–Mar

### DOOLIN, CO CLARE
**Aran View House (€–€€)**

This comfortable hotel is set in farmland.

✉ Coast Road ☎ 065 707 4061; www.aranview.com ⏱ Closed end Oct–Easter

### GALWAY, CO GALWAY
**Glenlo Abbey (€€€)**

Occupying an 18th-century abbey in a landscaped estate overlooking a lough.

✉ Bushypark ☎ 091 526666; www.glenlo.com

### Radisson Blu Hotel and Spa (€€–€€€)

A product of Galway's Celtic Tiger days, this impressive city centre hotel offers affordable opulence. Spa is open to non-residents.

✉ Lough Atalia Road ☎ 091 538300; www.radissonhotelgalway.com

### ROUNDSTONE, CO GALWAY
**Eldon's (€–€€)**

A distinctive blue-and-yellow-painted building in this picturesque fishing village. Eldon's restaurant specializes in local seafood.

✉ Main Street ☎ 095 35933; www.eldons.ie ⏱ Closed Jan

## RESTAURANTS

### CLARENBRIDGE, CO GALWAY
**Paddy Burkes (€€)**

Famous as the focal point of the Clarenbridge Oyster Festival; no prizes for guessing the speciality dish.

✉ Clarenbridge ☎ 091 796226; www.paddyburkesgalway.com ⏱ Daily lunch, dinner

### CLIFDEN, CO GALWAY
**Mitchell's Restaurant (€€)**

Hearty Irish stew is the speciality here, with good portions of seafood and steaks from a varied menu.

✉ Market Street ☎ 095 21867 ⏱ Daily 12–10; closed mid-Nov to mid-Mar

## DONEGAL, CO DONEGAL
### Harbour Restaurant (€–€€)
Cosy restaurant with a good variety of international and Irish dishes.

✉ Quay Street ☎ 074 972 1702; www.theharbour.ie ⏰ Daily 4–10

## GALWAY, CO GALWAY
### K C Blakes (€–€€)
John Casey (K C) is the larger-than-life owner of this ultramodern little eatery. Dishes range from traditional Irish with a twist to classic French and oriental.

✉ 10 Quay Street, Spanish Arch ☎ 091 561826 ⏰ Daily 5–10

### Kirbys of Cross Street (€–€€)
Good-value contemporary cuisine on Irish themes, seasoned with influences from further afield.

✉ Cross Street ☎ 091 563377; www.buskerbrownes.com ⏰ Daily lunch, dinner

### Kirwan's Lane Restaurant (€€–€€€)
Stylish modern restaurant serving bistro-type grills and Asian-influenced dishes.

✉ Kirwan's Lane ☎ 091 568266 ⏰ Mon–Sat lunch, dinner, Sun dinner May–Sep only

## KILCOLGAN, CO GALWAY
### Morans Oyster Cottage (€–€€€)
Famous for its seafood. Specialities include chowder and smoked salmon.

✉ The Weir ☎ 091 796113; www.moransoystercottage.com
⏰ Mon–Thu 12–11:30, Fri–Sat 12–12, Sun 12–11

## LETTERFRACK, CO GALWAY
### Rosleague Manor (€€€)
You have to make a reservation to eat in the classy restaurant of this stunning Georgian house, set in 12ha (30 acres) overlooking Ballinakill Bay. Seafood is the speciality.

✉ Letterfrack ☎ 095 41101; www.rosleague.com 🕐 Daily lunch, dinner; closed Nov to mid-Mar

## LISDOONVARNA, CO CLARE
### Sheedy's Country House Hotel (€€€)
Set in lovely gardens, this family-run hotel-restaurant has an excellent reputation for its food and hospitality.

✉ Lisdoonvarna ☎ 065 707 4026; www.sheedys.com 🕐 Daily lunch (bar meals), dinner; closed mid-Oct to Easter

## MOYCULLEN, CO GALWAY
### White Gables Restaurant (€€€)
This charming restaurant has an excellent reputation for its French cuisine and seafood.

✉ Moycullen village ☎ 091 555744; www.whitegables.com 🕐 Wed–Sat from 7pm, Sun from 12:30pm; closed 23 Dec to mid-Feb

## OILEÁIN ÁRANN (ARAN ISLANDS), CO GALWAY
### Mainistir House (€)
Come here for a quirky dining experience overlooking the bay. The daily changing set menu is sure to please.

✉ Inis Mór (Inishmore) ☎ 099 61169; www.mainistirhousearan.com 🕐 Daily: dinner at 8pm (one sitting only; booking essential)

## RECESS, CO GALWAY
### Ballynahinch Castle (€€–€€€)
Local game, fish and fresh produce inspire the menu here.

✉ On Roundstone road, off N59, 5km (3 miles) west of Recess ☎ 095-31006; www.ballynahinch-castle.com 🕐 Daily lunch (bar meals), dinner; closed 29 Jan–23 Feb and 15–27 Dec

## ROUNDSTONE, CO GALWAY
### O'Dowd's Seafood Bar and Restaurant (€€–€€€)
Traditional pub with restaurant serving excellent Irish cooking prepared using fresh locally caught fish.

✉ Roundstone ☎ 095 35809; www.odowdsbar.com 🕐 Bar food: daily 12–9:30. Restaurant: Apr–Sep daily 12–10; Oct–Mar 12–3, 6–9:30

## SLIGO, CO SLIGO
### Embassy Wine Bar and Grill and The Belfry (€–€€)
Renowned for both its à la carte and its bar food.

✉ John F Kennedy Parade ☎ 071 916 1250; www.embassygrill.eu
🕐 Restaurant: Tue–Sat 5–10, Sun 12:30–2:30, 5–10. Belfry pub: Mon–Fri
from 10:30am, Sat–Sun from 12:30pm

### Fiddlers Creek (€€–€€€)
Good, wholesome steak and fish dishes served with an interesting
slant. Some tables overlook the river.

✉ Rockwood Parade ☎ 071 914 1866; www.fiddlerscreek.ie 🕐 Daily
12:30–3:30, 5–late

## WESTPORT, CO MAYO
### Asgard Bar and Restaurant (€€–€€€)
Overlooking Clew Bay; good seafood and Irish specialities.

✉ The Quay ☎ 098 25319 🕐 Daily lunch, dinner; Sat–Sun only in winter

# SHOPPING

## CRAFTS
### Ballycasey Craft & Design Centre
Craftspeople here include potters, a goldsmith, a florist and more.

✉ Shannon, Co Clare ☎ 061 364115

### Burren Perfumery
Demonstrations, displays, photographic exhibition and tea rooms.

✉ Carron, Co Clare ☎ 065 708 9102 🕐 Jul–Aug daily 9–7; May–Jun, Sep
10–6; Oct–Apr 10–5; Jan by appointment only

### Donegal Craft Village
Variety of items, including pottery, uilleann pipes, jewellery, batik
and woven goods. Coffee shop.

✉ Ballyshannon Road, Donegal, Co Donegal ☎ 074 972 2225 🕐 Mon–Sat
10–5:30 (sometimes closed in winter)

### Doolin Crafts Gallery
Crafts gallery run by batik artist and jewellery designer. Also sells

weaving and Irish instruments. The on-site restaurant serves local produce.

✉ Doolin, Co Clare ☎ 065 707 4309 ◷ Daily (restaurant Apr–Oct)

## Foxford Woollen Mills Visitor Centre

Take a tour of the historic woollen mill. Also houses jewellery and woodcraft workshops and an art gallery.

✉ Foxford, Co Mayo ☎ 094 925 6104 ◷ May–Oct Mon–Sat 10–6, Sun 12–6; Nov–Apr Mon–Sat 10–6, Sun 2–6

## IDA Centre

Music, fashion and craft shops including pottery and jewellery. Bodhrán-making demonstrations. Café.

✉ Roundstone, Co Galway ☎ 095 35875

## DEPARTMENT STORES
### Brown Thomas

A western version of Dublin's most stylish shop. The place for luxury, perfume, designer clothes and accessory shopping.

✉ 18–21 Eglinton Buildings, Galway ☎ 091 565254 ◷ Mon, Wed, Sat 9:30–6:30, Tue 10–6:30, Thu–Fri 9:30–8, Sun 12–6

### Magee's

A legend in the world of department stores, run by the same family since 1866. The speciality is hand-woven Donegal tweed; guided tours of original looms at work.

✉ The Diamond, Donegal, Co Donegal ☎ 074 972 2660 ◷ Mon–Sat 9:30–6

### Penneys

Fashion for everyone (it's Primark in the UK); good accessories department and household wares.

✉ Eyre Square Centre, Galway, Co Galway ☎ 091 566889/565095

## TRADITIONAL MUSIC
### Custy's Traditional Music Shop

Owned and staffed by experts. A real gem.

✉ Cookes Lane, Ennis, Co Clare ☎ 065 682 1727; www.custysmusic.com

## ENTERTAINMENT

### LIVE MUSIC
#### Cuba/Bar 903
Latin American and jazz to hip hop, soul and funk.

✉ Eyre Square, Galway, Co Galway ☎ 091 565991 🕐 Nightly

#### The Roisin Dubh
Galway's main venue for touring bands, comedy and traditional acoustic music. Rooftop beer garden and bar.

✉ 8 Upper Dominick Street, Galway, Co Galway ☎ 091 586540
🕐 Nightly

#### Tigh Coilí
Traditional music venue in the heart of Galway's pedestrian area.

✉ Mainguard Street, Galway, Co Galway ☎ 091 561294 🕐 Nightly at 6 and 9:30

### NIGHTCLUBS
#### GPO
Established in 1994, this is the hippest and most popular dance club in the West.

✉ 36 Upper Abbeygate Street, Galway, Co Galway ☎ 091 563073;
www.gpo.ie 🕐 Mon–Wed 10pm–2am, Thu–Sun 11pm–3am

### PERFORMING ARTS
#### The Linenhall
A versatile arts centre bringing international performers to Mayo, as well as art-house cinema, drama and traditional Irish music.

✉ Linenhall Street, Castlebar, Co Mayo ☎ 094 902 3733;
www.thelinenhall.com

#### Town Hall Theatre
Drama, film, music of many styles and a roster of guest speakers from the literary world make this a worthwhile night out on the west of Ireland.

✉ Courthouses Square, Galway, Co Galway ☎ 091 569777; www.tht.ie

# Belfast and Northern Ireland

**Northern Ireland, so long notorious for "the Troubles", has benefited greatly from over a decade of peace. Tourists now throng to what is one of the most underrated parts of Ireland. Its beautiful scenery can match anything down south, but much of the region still feels undiscovered, and this only adds to the excitement of a visit and the warmness of the welcome you'll receive.**

Belfast

The coast of Antrim offers a spectacular drive past the lovely Glens before swinging west to the Giant's Causeway.

Further south the Mountains of Mourne sweep down to the sea. Inland are forest parks, lakes and mountains, historic towns, ancient sites and, of course, Belfast, a busy city with an industrial heritage and a lively arts scene.

## BELFAST

The capital of Northern Ireland is a relatively young city that grew rapidly in Victorian times, when its linen and shipbuilding industries flourished and the city doubled in size every 10 years. Today it has a unique character, brought about by the combination of hard work, hard times and a particular brand of Irish humour. The redevelopment of its dockyard areas continues to breathe new life and prosperity into the eastern flank of the city centre.

Belfast's industrial past, together with the disturbing images of the Troubles, can conjure up a somewhat misleading picture for those who have never visited the city. Its Victorian prosperity has left a legacy of magnificent public buildings and monuments, finance houses and warehouses. At the heart of the city is the spacious and leafy Donegall Square, dominated by the magnificent City Hall, and the whole area has undergone a huge makeover.

Belfast has superb museums, libraries and art galleries, excellent shopping and a lively and varied cultural life, from grand opera to informal traditional music sessions.

Beautiful parks and gardens include the famous Botanic Gardens and the canalside Lagan Valley Regional Park, but the most spectacular is on the slopes of Cave Hill to the north, which incorporates the zoo, Belfast Castle and a heritage centre.

✚ 10C

ℹ 47 Donegall Place ☎ 028 9024 6609

### Botanic Gardens

The Botanic Gardens are a wonderful place to wander away from the bustle of the city. You'll find a fragrant rose garden, formal beds and herbaceous borders, and among the outstanding greenhouses is the Palm House. Begun in 1839, it is a remarkable cast-iron, curvilinear structure in which tropical plants thrive. Also in these lovely surroundings, the **Ulster Museum** gives a fascinating insight into the life and history of the Province. Displays range from the dinosaurs, through ancient Egypt to artefacts from Ireland's troubled past and some important works of art.

✠ *Belfast 1f (off map)* ✉ Stranmills Road ☎ 028 9031 4762 ◷ Gardens: 7:30am–dusk. Palm House: Apr–Sep Mon–Fri 10–5, Sat–Sun 1–5; Oct–Mar Mon–Fri 10–3:45, Sat–Sun 1–3:45. Closes for lunch ✋ Free 🚌 Metro 7, Metro 8 🚉 Botanic Station

### Ulster Museum

☎ 0845 608 0000; www.nmni.com ◷ Tue–Sun 10–5 ✋ Free

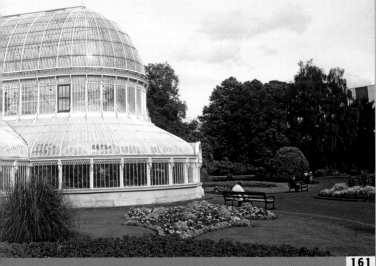

### City Hall

In 1906 Belfast's City Hall was completed to mark the granting of city status by Queen Victoria. Set around a central courtyard, the building, of Portland stone, is topped by a tall copper dome which rises above the central staircase at the heart of an exuberant interior of rich mosaic, stained glass, marble and wood panelling.

✚ *Belfast 2d* ✉ Donegall Square ☎ 028 9027 0456 ◷ Tours: Mon–Fri 11, 2, 3, Sat 2, 3 ✋ Free

### Crown Liquor Saloon

High Victorian decor is preserved in this pub, in the care of the National Trust. It's a working pub managed by a brewery. The tiled exterior, with Corinthian pillars flanking the doorway, gives way to marble counters, stained glass, gleaming brass and ornately carved "snugs".

✚ *Belfast 1e* ✉ 46 Great Victoria Street ☎ 028 9024 3187 ◷ Mon–Sat 11:30–12, Sun 11:30–10 ✋ Free

### Odyssey

Belfast's big millennium project was the building of this complex, completed in 2001, covering 9ha (22 acres) of the riverfront. It includes the W5 interactive science centre (www.w5online.co.uk), with a special area for kids under eight, a huge arena, and the Pavilion has restaurants, bars and shops, and a 12-screen multiplex cinema.

**www.**odysseypavilion.com

🚩 *Belfast 4b* ✉ 2 Queen's Quay ☎ 028 9045 1055

✋ Varies by attraction

### Queen's University

Northern Ireland's leading seat of third-level learning was founded by Queen Victoria and stands right at the heart of the city along eponymous University Road. The elegant, Charles Lanyon-designed, redbrick-and-sandstone, Tudor-revival building dates back to 1849, and it's three square towers have long been city landmarks. The university

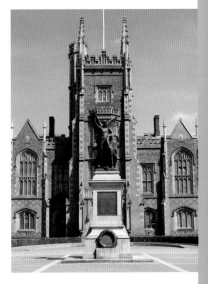

has grown a lot since then, but the enclosed campus is still a joy to stroll around and the Welcome Centre hosts regular exhibitions, as does the Naughton Art Gallery.

**www.**qub.ac.uk

🚩 *Belfast 1f (off map)* ✉ University Road ☎ 028 90975252 🕐 Welcome Centre: May–Sep Mon–Sat 9:30–4:30, Sun 10–1; Oct–Apr Mon–Fri 9:30–4:30

✋ Free

# a walk around Belfast

**This walk starts in the heart of the city, then heads south along "The Golden Mile" to visit the lovely Botanic Gardens and the Ulster Museum.**

Donegall Square is surrounded by splendid architecture. Take a look at some of the statues and monuments in the grounds of City Hall before going inside (guided tours can be arranged in advance).

*Leave by the exit on the opposite side. Outside the gates of City Hall turn left along Donegall Square South. At the corner cross into May Street, then turn right into Alfred Street. Continue to reach St Malachy's on the left.*

St Malachy's Church was built in 1844 in castellated Gothic style with dark red brick and slender octagonal turrets. Inside there is fine fan-vaulting and an organ by William Telford.

*From St Malachy's Church enter Clarence Street, turn left into Bedford Street, then bear right into Dublin Road and continue to Shaftesbury Square. Continue along Bradbury Place and fork left into University Road. Beyond the university, turn left to enter the Botanic Gardens, where the Ulster Museum can be found.*

The beautiful Botanic Gardens feature a great Palm House and Tropical Ravine. Nearby is the excellent Ulster Museum.

*Retrace your steps to Shaftesbury Square, then fork left to go along Great Victoria Street, passing the Crown Liquor Saloon on the right.*

Try to time your walk so that this famous National Trust pub, with its sumptuous and ornate Victorian interior, will be open.

*Continue past the Europa Hotel and the splendid Opera House, then turn right into Howard Street and return to Donegall Square.*

**Distance** About 4km (2.5 miles)
**Time** 3–4 hours, including cathedral, gardens and museum visits
**Start/end point** Donegall Square ✚ *Belfast 2d* 🚌 All city-centre buses
**Lunch** Crown Liquor Saloon (££, ➤ 162)

# Northern Ireland

### ARMAGH

Armagh has a heritage of national importance. Nearby Navan Fort was the ancient capital of the kings of Ulster, and in AD445 St Patrick built his first church on the site now occupied by St Patrick's Cathedral. From here the Irish were converted to Christianity and Armagh remains the ecclesiastical capital of Ireland. There has been much rebuilding of this Church of Ireland cathedral, but its core is medieval. There is also a Roman Catholic cathedral of St Patrick, finished in 1904, with a lavish interior of murals depicting Irish saints. **St Patrick's Trian** has an exhibition on the saint. St Patrick was born around AD390 in Britain, the son of a Romano-British official. At 16 he was kidnapped by pirates and sold into slavery in Ireland, but later escaped due, he claimed, to divine intervention. This prompted his training for the ministry in Britain, before returning to Ireland and establishing the Christian faith here.

The city has many other beautiful buildings on its old streets, and the region's history is explored at the **Navan Centre**, which incorporates the ancient fort site.

✚ 9D 🚌 251 from Belfast, 61 from Portadown 🚉 Portadown

**St Patrick's Trian**

✉ 40 English Street ☎ 028 3752 1801; www.saintpatrickstrian.com
🕓 Sep–Jun Mon–Sat 10–5, Sun 2–5; Jul–Aug Mon–Sat 10–5:30, Sun 2–6
💷 Moderate 🍴 Restaurant (£)

**Navan Centre and Fort**

✉ 81 Killylea Road ☎ 028 3752 1801 🕓 Apr–Sep daily 10–7; Oct–Mar 10–4 ♿ Moderate 🍽 Café (£)

## BALLYCASTLE

Ballycastle, Co Antrim's largest town, is a popular seaside resort surrounded by some of Ireland's loveliest scenery. Nearby is the Carrick-a-Rede Rope Bridge, suspended 24.5m (80ft) above the sea, linking the cliff top to a rocky island, and from the harbour there are trips to Rathlin Island, one of the best places for birdwatching in Ireland.

On the edge of the town are the ruins of **Bonamargy Friary,** founded around 1500 and the burial place of the MacDonnell chiefs. At the end of August each year, the Diamond, at the centre of the town, is crammed with stalls, entertainments and horse-dealing during the famous Oul' Lammas Fair. **Ballycastle Museum** is in the 18th-century courthouse, and there's a Seafront

Exhibition Centre with crafts and information.

➕ 10A 🚌 From Ballymoney Station 🚆 Ballymoney

**Bonamargy Friary**

✉ Ballycastle

🕓 All year ♿ Free

**Ballycastle Museum**

✉ 59 Castle Street

☎ 028 2076 2942

🕓 Jul–Aug (or by arrangement) Mon–Sat 12–6

♿ Free

## CARRICKFERGUS

Carrickfergus has Northern Ireland's finest Norman **castle,** built on the edge of the sea in the late 12th century and still in use (as a magazine and armoury) as recently as 1928. The Norman barons John de Courcy, then Hugh de Lacy, governed the mini Kingdom of Ulster from here before King John of England captured the castle following a siege in 1210. The castle was the focus for English rule in Ulster from then on, attracting the attentions of the Scottish, French and even John Paul Jones's American attackers at various times. Its walls now house three floors of exhibitions, and a medieval fair is held here each July.

The great square keep or tower at the centre of the castle is 27m (90ft) high, with walls over 2.5m (8ft) thick. On the ground floor is a well which draws water from 11m (36ft) below the castle, and a dungeon famous for the daring escape of one Con O'Neil of Clandboye in 1605. This Irish noble had been involved in a drunken brawl in which an English soldier had died. His wife smuggled him a rope hidden in a piece of cheese.

Carrickfergus was the first footfall in Ireland of William of Orange, who landed here in 1690 for his (ultimately victorious) campaign against James II. Billy's Rock reputedly marks the exact spot.

Visitors to Carrickfergus will be struck by the proximity of the huge Kilroot power station on the western side of town. It is Northern Ireland's last coal-fired power station, the fuel being brought in by boat to the long pier extending into Belfast Bay. An unusual and related attraction is **Flame! The Gasworks Museum of Ireland,** Ireland's sole surviving coal gasworks. It supplied Carrickfergus with gas for light and heating for more than 100 years until it closed in 1965. Visitors can climb to the top of the huge gasholder for an alternative view of this historic town.

✚ 10C 🚆 Carrickfergus

### Carrickfergus Castle

✉ Marine Highway ☎ 028 9335 1273 🕓 Easter–Sep daily 10–6; Oct–Easter 10–4 ✋ Inexpensive

### Flame! The Gasworks Museum of Ireland

✉ 44 Irish Quarter West ☎ 028 9336 9575 🕓 May–Aug Sun–Fri 2–5; Sep Mon–Fri 2–5. Other times by appointment ✋ Free

## CASTLE COOLE

This impressive Palladian mansion rises out of the meadows and parkland of the Fermanagh countryside. It was completed in 1798 for the Earl of Belmore, and the grounds and house are now in the hands of the National Trust. On the guided tours you can learn about the family's story, including how the sumptuous State Bedroom was prepared for a visit by George IV in 1821 but he never came, preferring the company of one of his mistresses instead. You can also glimpse the life of the staff 'below stairs' in a Great House, seeing the extensive servants' quarters in the basement.

www.nationaltrust.org.uk

✚ 7D ✉ Enniskillen, Co Fermanagh ☎ 028 6632 2690 🕓 House: Easter, Jul–Aug daily 11–5; May–Jun, Sep Fri–Wed 11–5; mid-Mar to Apr, Oct Sat–Sun 11–5. Last tour 1 hour before closing. Garden and park: Mar–Oct daily 10–7; Nov–Feb 10–4 ✋ House: moderate (guided tour only). Gardens: inexpensive 🚌 Ulsterbus 95 Enniskillen–Clones (connections to Belfast)

## ENNISKILLEN

Enniskillen is attractively set on the River Erne between Upper and Lower Lough Erne. **Enniskillen Castle,** built in the early 15th century, was the medieval stronghold of the Maguires and has a picturesque water gate. The keep now houses the Fermanagh Museum and a military museum. St Macartan's Cathedral is a small but interesting building, dating from the early 17th century, with some fine monuments and stained glass.

The Fermanagh Lakelands surrounding Enniskillen provide for all kinds of water-based leisure pursuits, and on Devenish Island is an important monastic site, founded in the 6th century by St Molaise.

A little farther afield is Castle Coole, designed by James Wyatt in 1795 (➤ 169). **Florence Court** is to the southwest, an 18th-century mansion noted for its rococo plasterwork.

✚ 7D

🚢 Ferry from Lower Lough Erne, north of Enniskillen, to Devenish Island

### Enniskillen Castle

✉ Castle Barracks, Wellington Road ☎ 028 6632 5000; www.enniskillencastle.co.uk ⏰ Mon 2–5, Tue–Fri 10–5. Also open Mar–Sep Sat 2–5 (also Sun 2–5 Jul–Aug) 💷 Inexpensive 🚌 261 from Belfast

### Florence Court

✉ 12km (7.5 miles) southwest of Enniskillen ☎ 028 6634 8249; www.nationaltrust.org.uk ⏰ House: Apr, Jul–Aug daily 11–5; May–Jun, Sep Wed–Mon 11–5; mid-Mar to Apr, Oct Sat–Sun 11–5. Grounds: Mar–Oct daily 10–7; Nov–Feb 10–4 💷 Moderate 🍴 Tea room (£) 🚌 Ulsterbus 192 Enniskillen–Swanlinbar

## THE GIANT'S CAUSEWAY

Best places to see, ➤ 42–43.

## THE GIANT'S CAUSEWAY COAST

The Giant's Causeway Coast encompasses dramatic cliffs, wide sandy beaches, pretty fishing villages and clifftop castles. Portrush, the nearest large town, is a traditional seaside resort with two splendid beaches, and nearby is **Dunluce Castle,** a fairy-tale ruin which seems to grow out of the rock on which it is perched. Portballintrae is a pretty fishing village, made famous by the discovery in 1967 of the most valuable sunken treasure ever found on an Armada wreck – the *Girona* – which foundered here in 1588, with only five survivors from its crew of 1,300. The rescued treasure is now on display and can be seen in Belfast's Ulster Museum (➤ 161).

➕ 9–10A

**Dunluce Castle**

✉ 87 Dunluce Road, Bushmills ☎ 028 2073 1938; www.ni-environment.gov.uk ⏰ Apr–Sep daily 10–6; Oct–Mar 10–4 ✋ Inexpensive 🚌 172 Portrush–Ballycastle

## THE GLENS OF ANTRIM

There are nine Glens of Antrim, lying roughly east of an imaginary line drawn between Ballycastle and Ballymena, and all of them are beautiful. There are wide valleys with a patchwork of green pastures, densely wooded mountain slopes and rocky gorges with tumbling streams dappled by the sunlight shining through the overhanging trees. Many of the glens are designated nature reserves and there are splendid walks, rich in wildlife and botanical interest and often with views to the coast. Millions of years of geological upheaval have formed these delightful valleys, which lie between the great plateau of the Antrim Mountains and a coastline that is justifiably described as the most scenic in the British Isles (➤ 174–175). Glenariff, the best known, has been dubbed the 'queen of the glens', and there is a wonderful view from the visitor centre. Glendun is known for the impressive Charles Lanyon viaduct, which carries the A2 over the River Dun.

✚ 10B

🛈 Sheskburn House, 7 Mary Street, Ballycastle ☎ 028 2076 2024

## LONDONDERRY

Londonderry (Derry) is a city that is historically absorbing, yet lively and modern too. Take a guided walk of about 1.5km (1 mile) around its 17th-century town walls, which are still unbroken in spite of a 105-day siege by Jacobite forces in 1689, one of the most significant battles in Irish history. The city has hardly ever been trouble-free. Ever since St Columba founded his first monastery here in AD546, its accessible location on the Foyle estuary attracted marauders. You can learn more of the history of the town at the **Tower Museum.**

Londonderry has impressive public buildings, two fine cathedrals and dramatic townscapes, but there are also lots of little lanes to explore, and behind the 19th-century Guildhall is the quay from which so many emigrants sailed for the New World.

✚ 8B

**Tower Museum**

✉ Union Hall Place ☎ 028 7137 2411; www.derrycity.gov.uk 🕐 Tue–Sat 10–5 (last admission 4:30) ✋ Inexpensive 🚉 Londonderry

# a drive around the Antrim coast

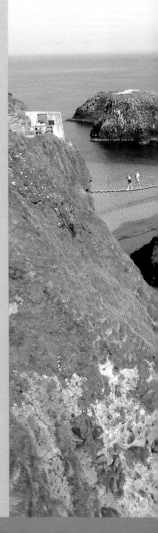

*From Larne take the A2 north signed Glenarm and the Antrim Coast Road.*

All the way to Ballycastle you will pass wonderful coastal scenery and pretty villages. Turn off to explore the Glens of Antrim if you have time.

*Pass Bonamargy Friary on the left and at the T-junction turn left into Ballycastle. From the Diamond take the A2 signposted Portrush, Bushmills, Giant's Causeway. Soon turn right, signposted Ballintoy, B15, Coastal Route. At the T-junction turn right and continue, passing the turning to Carrick-a-Rede Rope Bridge.*

In summer the rope bridge is strung high above the water across the gap between the mainland and a little rocky island.

*Go through Ballintoy and after 5.5km (3.5 miles) turn right into Causeway Road. After another 5.5km (3.5 miles) you reach the Visitor Centre.*

This is a World Heritage Site and an amazing phenomenon which should not be missed.

*From the Causeway, take the A2 to Bushmills and at the roundabout in the village go straight over, signposted Dervock. After a short distance, reach the Bushmills Distillery on the left.*

Though it is a large-scale working distillery, Bushmills is well prepared for visitors, with an interesting and entertaining tour, tastings and shops.

*Continue to Dervock, then at a T-junction turn right with the B66, signposted Ballymoney. About 6.5km (4 miles) farther on turn left onto the A26. Stay on this road and at the end of its short motorway section, reach a roundabout and turn left onto the A36. From here follow signs back to Larne.*

**Distance** 160km (100 miles)
**Time** About 7 hours
**Start/end point** Larne ✚ 10B
**Lunch** The Nook, Giant's Causeway, tel 028 2073 2993

## LOUGH NEAGH

Lough Neagh, the largest lake in the British Isles, has little hidden harbours, sandy beaches and a number of islands. Lakes are always best explored by boat, and Lough Neagh is no exception, because the roads around it rarely follow the waterline. The *Irish Mist* cruises around the lake from the marina at Antrim, a busy and attractive town, with a famous 9th-century round tower.

In the southeastern corner of the lough, Oxford Island has a range of habitats for birdlife, including wet meadows, reedbeds, woodlands and shoreline scrub. The **Lough Neagh Discovery Centre** here has audio-visual shows and interactive games, and visitors can participate in guided walks or take a boat trip.

For more seclusion, there are hides (camouflaged shelters) for birdwatching and a variety of marked walking trails.

✚ 9C

**Lough Neagh Discovery Centre**

✉ Oxford Island ☎ 028 3832 2205 🕐 Jul–Aug Mon–Fri 9–6, Sat–Sun 10–6; Sep–Jun Mon–Fri 9–5, Sat–Sun 10–6 💰 Free 🍴 Cafe (££)

## MOUNTAINS OF MOURNE

Percy French wrote many popular songs extolling the beauty of Ireland, but his best-known line must surely be *"where the Mountains of Mourne sweep down to the sea"*. Few first-time visitors, though, would be prepared for the wild beauty of the scenery.

The **Mourne Heritage Trust** at Newcastle is a good place to start, with lots of useful information and guided walks. One of the nature trails follows the "Brandy Pad", a notorious smugglers' route that links Hilltown, notable for its many pubs, with the coast south of Newcastle.

Slieve Donard, at 839m (2,752ft), is the highest mountain, and clothing its slopes is the Donard Forest Park. There is more woodland to explore in the Tollymore and Castlewellan forest parks, while to the south is the evocatively named Silent Valley, which was flooded in 1922 to form two great reservoirs. There is a charge for cars to enter the forest parks and Silent Valley, which are accessible from about 10am (closing time varies depending on the season).

➕ 10D

### Mourne Heritage Trust

✉ 87 Central Promenade, Newcastle ☎ 028 4372 4059; www.mournelive.com 🕐 Mon–Fri 9–5 ✋ Free

## MOUNT STEWART HOUSE AND GARDENS

One of Ireland's grandest stately homes, Mount Stewart was built for the 3rd Marquess of Londonderry. Three architects were involved in the building – James Wyatt, in the 1780s, then George Dance and (probably) William Vitruvious Morrison in the early 19th century. The imposing interior largely reflects the impeccable taste of the 7th Marchioness, a leader of London society in the 1920s and 1930s. She was also responsible for the garden, which benefits from the mild climate between the Irish Sea and Strangford Lough.

**www.**nationaltrust.org.uk

➕ 11C ✉ 8km (5 miles) southeast of Newtownards ☎ 028 4278 8387
🎟 Lakeside gardens: daily 10–6. Formal gardens: mid-Mar to Oct daily 10–6. House: mid-Mar to Oct Thu–Tue 11–6 ✋ Moderate 🍴 Tea room (£)
🚌 Ulsterbus 9 and 10 from Belfast–Portaferry 🚉 Bangor

## ULSTER AMERICAN FOLK PARK

Best places to see, ➤ 54–55.

## ULSTER FOLK AND TRANSPORT MUSEUM

All kinds of Ulster buildings have been painstakingly dismantled in their original locations, brought to this 25ha (62-acre) site and reconstructed in appropriate settings, including a small town of the 1900s, complete with shops, a school, churches, printer's workshops, a bank and terraced (row) houses. Rural exhibits include traditional Irish cottages, watermills and farmhouses, and farming is represented by rare breeds of animals, and fields which are cultivated using traditional methods.

The Transport Museum is comprehensive, covering all forms of transport from horse-drawn carts to the De Lorean car, and

includes the superb Irish Railway Collection and the X2 Flight Experience, an interactive exhibition. Perennially popular is the *Titanic* exhibition, about the 'unsinkable' liner which was built in Belfast's shipyards and foundered after hitting an iceberg on its maiden voyage. As well as the permanent exhibitions, the museum has special events, which change from year to year.

**www.**nmni.com

🏠 10C ✉ Bangor Road, Cultra, Holywood ☎ 028 9042 8428 🕐 Mar–Sep Tue–Sun 10–5; Oct–Feb Tue–Fri 10–4, Sat–Sun 11–4; open Bank Holiday Mondays throughout year 🖐 Moderate 🍴 Tea room (£) 🚌 B1, B2 from Belfast to Bangor 🚉 Cultra Halt

## WELLBROOK BEETLING MILL

This water-powered, 18th-century linen hammer mill, set in a lovely wooded glen on the banks of the fast-flowing River Ballinderry, is a testament to the history of linen-making in Northern Ireland. For much of the 19th century the north of Ireland was the world's greatest producer of linen and you can see demonstrations of how the material was made.

Tours are conducted around the mill, costumed interpreters explain the process of manufacture and you can try your hand at scutching, hackling, weaving and beetling. Beetling is the final process in linen manufacture, when the cloth is repeatedly hammered to produce a sheen – the heavy wooden hammers used were known as beetles. The process could last for anything between two days and two weeks. The mill's seven water-powered beetling engines create a thunderous noise and it was not unusual for the beetlers to become completely or partially deaf working in a confined space for up to 15 hours a day.

**www.**nationaltrust.org.uk

🏠 8C ✉ Wellbrook Road, Corkhill (6.5km/4 miles west of Cookstown) ☎ 028 8675 1735 🕐 Jul–Aug Sat–Thu 2–6; Mar–Jun, Sep Sat–Sun 2–6; Easter Fri–Tue 1–6 🖐 Moderate 🚌 Ulsterbus 80 from Cookstown; request stop at Kildress then 1km (half-mile) walk ❓ Shop; scenic walks

## HOTELS

### ARMAGH, CO ARMAGH
**Hillview Lodge (£)**
Family-run guest house with good facilities in a rural setting just
1.5km (1 mile) from the city. Golf driving range.
✉ 33 Newtownhamilton Road ☎ 028 3752 2000; www.hillviewlodge.com

### BALLINTOY, CO ANTRIM
**Whitepark House (££)**
Country house on the coast road between the Causeway and the
rope bridge.
✉ 150 Whitepark Road ☎ 028 2073 1482; www.whiteparkhouse.com

### BELFAST, CO ANTRIM
**Hastings Europa Hotel (£££)**
The Europa is a truly international hotel with excellent facilities and
was the choice of President Clinton during his visits to Belfast in
1995 and 1998. It was once famed for being 'the most bombed
hotel' but can now be described as luxurious.
✉ Great Victoria Street ☎ 028 9027 1066; www.hastingshotel.com

**Jury's Inn Belfast (£–££)**
In the heart of the city, next to the Opera House, a short walk from
the main shopping area.
✉ Fisherwick Place, Great Victoria Street ☎ 028 9053 3500;
www.jurysinns.com

**Malone Lodge Hotel (££)**
A friendly town house hotel, close to the University and the Ulster
Museum, with a range of good eating options too.
✉ 60 Eglantine Avenue ☎ 028 9038 8000; www.malonelodgehotelbelfast.com

### CARNLOUGH, CO ANTRIM
**Londonderry Arms Hotel (££–£££)**
Famous for its food and its history, this fine Georgian house was
once owned by Sir Winston Churchill.
✉ 20 Harbour Road ☎ 028 2888 5255; www.glensofantrim.com

### COLERAINE, CO LONDONDERRY
**Breezemount House (£–££)**
Restored 19th-century house offering superior bed-and-breakfast facilities. Rooms have private bathroom, kitchen and satellite TV.
✉ 26 Castlerock Road ☎ 028 7034 4615; www.breezemount.co.uk

### ENNISKILLEN, CO FERMANAGH
**Killyhevlin Hotel (£)**
With dreamy views across the upper reaches of Lough Erne, the Killyhevlin is a great base for touring Fermanagh and the border country. Self-catering chalets are also available.
✉ Killyhevlin, Enniskillen ☎ 028 6632 3481; www.killyhevlin.com

### LONDONDERRY, CO LONDONDERRY
**The Merchant's House (£)**
This Victorian merchant's family home has been converted into one of the city's finest bed-and-breakfasts.
✉ 16 Queen Street ☎ 028 7126 9691; www.thesaddlershouse.com

## RESTAURANTS

### ANNALONG, CO DOWN
**Glassdrumman Lodge (£££)**
Prime local produce, including prawns and salmon, feature on the six-course dinner menu of well-produced dishes.
✉ 85 Mill Road ☎ 028 4376 8451 🕙 Mon–Sat 7–9, Sun 12:30–2:30, 7–9

### BALLYMENA, CO ANTRIM
**Galgorm Resort and Spa (£££)**
The restaurant of this restored 19th-century mansion offers fine dining overlooking the River Maine.
✉ 136 Fenaghy Road ☎ 028 2588 1001 🕙 Daily lunch, dinner

### BANGOR, CO DOWN
**Jeffers by the Marina (£–££)**
Bustling bistro, facing Bangor's waterfront gardens, serving local ingredients with a Mediterranean twist.
✉ 7 Grays Hill ☎ 028 9185 9555 🕙 Tue–Sat 10–10, Sun 11–8

## BELFAST, CO ANTRIM
### Morning Star (££)
An historic Belfast pub with exceptionally good food, using only the freshest Ulster produce and seafood.
✉ 17 Pottinger's Entry ☎ 028 9032 5986 🕐 Daily from 12

### Nick's Warehouse (£–££)
See page 59.

### The Northern Whig (£–££)
Caesar salad, beef and Guinness sausages, salmon goujons and more served in this old printing press-turned-stylish restaurant.
✉ 2 Bridge Street ☎ 028 9050 9888 🕐 Mon–Sat 12–9, Sun 1–8

## BUSHMILLS, CO ANTRIM
### The Nook (£)
Occupying a former school house next to the Giant's Causeway Visitor Centre, this is the perfect spot for a bit to eat or a quick drink after seeing the World Heritage Site.
✉ 48 Causeway Road ☎ 028 2073 2993 🕐 Daily 10am–11pm

## ENNISKILLEN, CO FERMANAGH
### Killyhevlin Hotel (£–££)
Excellent food and wonderful views over Lough Erne.
✉ Dublin Road, Killyhevlin ☎ 028 6632 3481 🕐 Breakfast, lunch, dinner

## HILLSBOROUGH, CO DOWN
### Hillside Restaurant and Bar (££)
Traditional country-house cooking with global influences.
✉ 21 Main Street ☎ 028 9268 9233; www.hillsidehillsborough.co.uk
🕐 Mon–Thu 12–9, Fri–Sat 12–9:30, Sun 12–8:30

## KILLYLEAGH, CO DOWN
### Dufferin Arms (£–££)
European, seafood and vegetarian choices feature heavily on the menu at this well-known country pub.
✉ 35 High Street ☎ 028 4482 1182 🕐 Lunch, dinner

### LIMAVADY, CO LONDONDERRY
#### The Lime Tree (££)
Modern Irish cuisine using the best of seasonal local produce.
Early-bird menus are particularly good value.
✉ 60 Catherine Street ☎ 028 7776 4300; www.limetreerest.com ✦ Dinner
only Tue–Sat

### LONDONDERRY, CO LONDONDERRY
#### Beech Hill Country House Hotel (££–£££)
This exclusive hotel, in a peaceful location in 13ha (32 acres) of
glorious woodlands, has an excellent restaurant serving fine local
ingredients such as dry-aged beef, hand-picked mussels and
Tyrone cheeses.
✉ 32 Ardmore Road ☎ 028 7134 9279; www.beech-hill.com ✦ Breakfast,
lunch, dinner

### OMAGH, CO TYRONE
#### Mellon Country Hotel (££)
The Mellon serves up traditional Irish cuisine with a modern twist.
✉ 134 Beltany Road ☎ 028 8166 1224; www.melloncountryhotel.com
✦ Lunch, dinner

### PORTAFERRY, CO DOWN
#### Portaferry Hotel (£££)
A charming 18th-century inn picturesquely set on the edge of
Strangford Lough. The restaurant is best known for its seafood.
✉ 10 The Strand ☎ 028 4272 8231; www.portaferryhotel.com ✦ Lunch,
early evening menu, à la carte dinner

# SHOPPING

## CRAFTS
### An Creagan
The craft shop at the Sperrins Visitor Centre specializes in locally
produced goods, including pottery, jewellery, and slate and
bronze items.
✉ Creggan, Omagh, Co Tyrone ☎ 028 8076 1112; www.an-creagan.com
✦ Mon–Fri 11–5:30, Sat–Sun 11–5

### Derry Craft Village

Craftspeople ply their trade in an 18th-century setting.

✉ Shipquay Street, Londonderry, Co Londonderry ☎ 028 7126 0329

🕔 Daily 9–6 or 7

### Gilmartins

In the border pottery village of Belleek, Gilmartins specializes in Irish crafts, including Belleek ware, Newbridge silver and iconic Irish signposts.

✉ 9 Main Street, Belleek, Co Fermanagh ☎ 028 6865 8371; www.gilmartinscraftshop.com 🕔 Mon–Sat 9:30–6

### SpaceCRAFT

Owned and run by the Craft and Design Collective, this city-centre store acts as both a shop and en exhibition space for members, who include photographers, artists, ceramicists, jewellers and furniture makers in their eclectic ranks.

✉ 9b The Fountain Centre, College Street, Belfast ☎ 028 9032 9342; www.craftanddesigncollective.com 🕔 Mon–Sat 10:30–5:30

### The Wicker Man

Highly regarded craft shop showcasing work by over 150 Irish craftspeople.

✉ 44–46 High Street, Belfast ☎ 028 9024 3550; www.thewickerman.co.uk

🕔 Mon–Wed, Sat 9–6, Thu 9–9, Sun 11–5:30

## SHOPPING CENTRES

### Victoria Centre

On four floors with more than 90 shops, this is one of Ireland's largest retail malls. All the usual British retailers are represented, along with restaurants, a cinema, bars and children's activities.

✉ 1 Victoria Square, Belfast ☎ 028 9032 2277; www.victoriasquare.com

🕔 Mon–Tue, Sat 9:30–6, Wed–Fri 9:30–9, Sun 1–6

## MARKETS

### Belmont Farmers' Market

Locally produced fruit and vegetables, bread, cheeses and even olives are on sale in this popular market beneath the Gothic Belmont Tower.

✉ 82 Belmont Church Road, Belfast ☎ 028 9065 3338; www.belmont-tower.co.uk ◷ Sat 9–1

### St George's Market

Built in 1896, the market has had a face-lift in recent years and is now one of the UK's finest. Saturday specializes in food.

✉ 10–20 East Bridge Street, Belfast ☎ 028 9032 0202 ◷ Fri 6am–2pm, Sat 9–3

## TRADITIONAL MUSIC
### Premier Record Store

Specializes in traditional CDs and tapes. Behind Castle Court Shopping Centre.

✉ 3–5 Smithfield Square North, Belfast ☎ 028 9024 0896 ◷ Mon–Sat 9–5:30

# ENTERTAINMENT

## LIVE MUSIC
### Dungloe Bar

Reliable Derry city music pub with local bands, traditional music and good *craic*.

✉ Waterloo Street, Londonderry, Co Londonderry ☎ 028 7126 7716

### John Hewitt Bar

In the heart of the Cathedral quarter, this interesting gastro pub stages jazz on Friday and traditional music on Tuesday, Wednesday and Saturday, blues on Thursday, open mic on Monday.

✉ 51 Donegall Street, Belfast ☎ 028 9023 3768

### Kitchen Bar

Live music here ranges from traditional Irish on a Saturday afternoon, to acoustic sessions on Sunday afternoons and bands Thursday to Saturday evenings, all accompanied by Paddy's soda bread pizza and a friendly atmosphere.

✉ 1 Victoria Square, Belfast ☎ 028 9024 5268

### Odyssey Arena

Belfast's biggest venue, for boy bands, pop sensations, classical interludes and the dinosaurs of rock. Ice shows, comedy and even WWE wrestling also make the bill.

✉ 2 Queen's Quay, Belfast ☎ 028 9073 9074; www.odysseyarena.com

## NIGHTCLUBS
### Front Page

Pub club with live bands – indie, techno and punk.

✉ Lower Donegall Street, Belfast ☎ 028 9032 4924

### Rain

One of Belfast's most popular clubs, offering dance music, decor and drink to suit a wide range of tastes.

✉ 10–14 Tomb Street, Belfast ☎ 028 9032 7308; www.rainnightclub.co.uk
🕑 Nightly

## PERFORMING ARTS
### Grand Opera House

Magnificent listed venue showing opera, musical theatre and ballet, as well as smaller productions in the Baby Grand.

✉ Great Victoria Street, Belfast ☎ 028 9023 6842; www.goh.co.uk

### Nerve Centre

Innovative, multimedia arts centre.

✉ 7–8 Magazine Street, Londonderry ☎ 028 7126 0562;
www.nerve-centre.org.uk

### Queen's Film Theatre

Shows the best in new and classic world cinema.

✉ 20 University Square Mews, Belfast ☎ 023 9097 1097;
www.queensfilmtheatre.com

### Verbal Arts Centre

Children's events, storytelling and more in the First Derry School by the city walls.

✉ London Street, Londonderry ☎ 028 7126 6946; www.verbalartstheatre.co.uk

# Sight locator index

This index relates to the maps on the covers. We have given map references to the main sights of interest in the book. Grid references in italics indicate sights featured on the town plans. Some sights within towns may not be plotted on the maps.

# Index

# Acknowledgements

The Automobile Association would like to thank the following photographers and companies for their assistance in the preparation of this book.

Abbreviations for the picture credits are as follows – (t) top; (b) bottom; (c) centre; (l) left; (r) right; (AA) AA World Travel Library

**4l** Dunmanus Bay, Co Cork, AA/J Blandford; **4c** Ferries at Rosslare, AA/C Jones; **4r** St Candice Cathedral, Kilkenny, AA/M Short; **5l** Ha'Penny Bridge, over River Liffey, Dublin, © Ingolf Pompe 64/Alamy; **5c** Powerscourt Estate, AA/L Blake; **6/7** Dunmanus Bay, Co Cork, AA/J Blandford; **8/9** St Colman's Cathedral, Cobh, AA/D Forss; **10/11t** O'Connell Street, Dublin, AA/S Day; **10cl** Rock of Cashel, AA/S McBride; **10cr** Dingle, AA/C Jones; **11c** Bar, Dublin, AA/S Whitehorne; **11b** Pony trap, Muckross estate, AA/J Blandford; **12b** Powerscourt Shopping Centre, Dublin, AA/M Short; **13tr** English Market, Cork, AA/S Hill; **13c** Food market, Dublin, AA/S Day; **14l** St Patrick's Street, Cork, AA/C Jones; **14r** Old Jameson Distillery, Dublin, AA/S Day; **15t** Guinness, AA/C Coe; **15b** Dublin, AA/S Day; **16/17t** Grafton Street, Dublin, AA/S Day; **16/17c** The Curragh, AA/C Coe; **16b** Derrynane and the Ring of Kerry, AA/J Blandford; **17b** Cliffs of Moher, AA/C Hill; **18** Giant's Causeway, AA/C Hill; **19t** Galway Oyster Festival, AA/S McBride; **19b** Athlone Castle, AA/L Blake; **20/21** Ferries at Rosslare, AA/C Jones; **25** Galway oyster festival, AA/S McBride; **27** Lough Leane, Co Kerry, AA/J Blandford; **28** Road between Glengarriff and Kenmare, AA; **29** Road signs, AA/M Diggin; **32/33** Garda car, AA/I Dawson; **34/35** St Canice Cathedral, Kilkenny, AA/M Short; **36/37t** Inscribed stones, AA/M Short; **36/37b** Newgrange, AA/M Short; **37cl** Mace head, Knowth, AA/C Coe; **38bl** Nun's Church, AA/C Coe; **38/39** Clonmacnoise, AA/L Blake; **39tr** Bay near Clonmacnoise, AA/S McBride; **40t** Dingle, AA/C Jones; **40c** Stone cross, Kilmalkedar Church, AA/C Jones; **41** Slea head, Dingle peninsula, AA/C Jones; **42/43** Giant's Causeway, AA/C Coe; **44cl** Kilkenny, AA/S Hill; **44c** Muckross House, AA/M Short; **44/45** Killarney Castle, AA/C Jones; **46** Muckross House, AA/J Blandford; **46/47b** Muckross House, K Welsh/Alamy; **48/49t** National Museum, AA/S Whitehorne; **48b** National Museum, AA/S Day; **50t** Celtic cross, Inishmore, AA/S Hill; **50c** Dun Aengus, Inishmore Island, AA/S Hill; **51** Collecting seaweed, AA/Stephen Hill; **52** Rock of Cashel, AA/S McBride; **53tl** Shamrock motif, Rock of Cashel, AA/S McBride; **53tr** Tomb, Rock of Cashel, AA/S McBride; **54/55t** 19th-century street of shops, Ulster American Folk Park; **54c** Mellon farmhouse, Ulster-American Folk Park; **56/57** Ha'Penny Bridge, over River Liffey, Dublin, © Ingolf Pompe 64/Alamy; **58** Restaurant, Dublin, AA/S McBride; **61** Dublin Castle, Record Tower, AA/S Day; **62/63** Connemara National Park, AA/C Jones; **65** Golfers, Ballybunion, AA/P Zollier; **66/67** Lough Erne, Co Kerry, AA/C Coe; **68** Belleek Pottery workshop, AA/J Johnson; **70/71bg** Viking Splash Tour, AA/S Day; **73** Fitzsimon's Inn, Dublin, AA/S Day; **74** Christ Church Cathedral, AA/S Whitehorne; **75tl** Dublin Castle, AA/S Day; **75tr** Temple Bar, AA/S Day; **77** Shaw Birthplace, Dublin, AA/S Day; **78/79** Powerscourt Estate, AA/L Blake; **81** South cross, Kells, AA/P Zollier; **83t** Record Tower, Dublin Castle, AA/S Day; **83b** Brendan Behan's typewriter, AA/S Day; **84** Atrium, Guinness Storehouse, **85t** Guinness Storehouse; **85b** Kilmainham Gaol AA/S Whitehorne; **86** National Gallery, AA/Slide File; **87** Old Jameson Distillery, AA/S Day; **88l** Trinity College, AA/L Blake; **88/89** The Old Library, AA; **90/91** Castletown House, AA/M Short; **92t** Glendalough, AA/C Jones; **92cb** Glendalough, AA/C Jones; **93b** Irish National Heritage Park, AA/P Zollier; **94l** Jerpoint Abbey, AA/M Short; **95t** Japanese Gardens, AA/S McBride; **95c** Japanese Gardens, AA/M Short; **96/97** Malahide Castle, AA/Slide File; **97r** Cross of Muiredach, AA/C Jones; **98tr** Powerscourt Gardens, AA/M Short; **100/101** Powerscourt, AA/M Short; **102** Lough Tay, Wicklow Mountains, AA/C Jones; **111** Cork, AA/S McBride; **112** St Finbarr's Cathedral and South Gate Bridge, AA/C Jones; **113r** Tribute to Rory Gallagher, AA/C Jones; **115** St Anne's Church, K Welsh/Alamy; **116** Bridge in Cork, AA/J Blandford; **117** St Patrick's Street, AA/J Blandford; **118t** Bantry Bay, AA/M Diggin; **118b** Garinish Island, AA/J Blandford; **119** Blarney Castle, AA/S McBride; **120/121** Rock of Cashel, AA/S McBride; **122l** Ring of Kerry, AA/J Blandford; **122/123** Jaunting car, Gap of Dunloe, AA/S McBride; **123r** Killarney, AA/J Blandford; **124/125** Killarney National Park, AA/S McBride; **126t** Kinsale, AA/D Forss; **126c** Kinsale, AA/S McBride; **127** Limerick, AA/P Zollier; **128** Christ Church Cathedral Precinct, AA/M Short; **137** The Burren, AA/S McBride; **138** Cathedral of Our Lady Assumed into Heaven and St Nicholas, AA/C Hill; **140** Galway City, © Vincent MacNamara/Alamy; **141** Statue of Padraic O Conaire, Eyre Square, AA/S McBride; **142** Bunratty Castle, AA/P Zollier; **143** The Burren, AA/S McBride; **144/145** Connemara National Park, AA/C Hill; **145br** Aughanure Castle, AA/C Jones; **146/147** Donegal Castle, Paul Mayall/Alamy; **148/149** Kylemore Abbey, AA/L Blake; **149br** King John's Castle, Athlone, AA/L Blake; **150t** Sligo, AA/I Dawson; **150/151b** Westport House, AA/L Blake; **151r** Thoor Ballylee, AA/S McBride; **159** Glenarm, AA/D Forss; **160** Waterfront area, Belfast, AA/C Coe; **161** Palm House, Botanic Gardens, AA/G Munday; **162t** City Hall, AA/I Dawson; **162b** Crown Liquor Saloon, AA/I Dawson; **163** Queen's University, Belfast, © J Orr/Alamy; **164** Ulster Museum, AA; **165t** Grand Opera House, AA/G Munday; **166** Palace stables, Armagh, AA/I Dawson; **167b** Fair Head from Ballycastle Bay, AA/M Diggin; **168** Carrickfergus Castle, AA/D Forss; **171** Dunluce Castle, AA/C Coe; **172t** Waterfall in Glenariff, AA/C Coe; **173c** Peace statue, Londonderry, AA/C Coe; **174/175** Carrick-a-Rede Rope Bridge, AA/G Munday; **176** Lough Neagh, AA/G Munday; **177** Tollymore Forest Park, AA; **178** Mount Stewart, AA/G Munday.

Every effort has been made to trace the copyright holders, and we apologise in advance for any accidental errors. We would be happy to apply the corrections in the following edition of this publication.

# Questionnaire

**Dear Traveler**

Your comments, opinions and recommendations are very important to us.
So please help us to improve our travel guides by taking a few minutes to
complete this simple questionnaire.

*Send to:* Essential Guides,
MailStop 64, 1000 AAA Drive, Heathrow, FL 32746–5063

Your recommendations...

We always encourage readers' recommendations for restaurants, nightlife
or shopping – if your recommendation is added to the next edition of the
guide, we will send you a FREE AAA Essential Guide of your choice.
Please state below the establishment name, location and your reasons for
recommending it.

_____

_____

_____

_____

_____

**Please send me AAA Essential** _____

About this guide...

Which title did you buy?

_____ **AAA Essential**

Where did you buy it? _____

When? m m / y y

Why did you choose a AAA Essential Guide? _____

_____

_____

Did this guide meet with your expectations?

Exceeded ☐   Met all ☐   Met most ☐   Fell below ☐

Please give your reasons _____

_____

_____

_____

continued on next page...

Were there any aspects of this guide that you particularly liked? _____

_____

_____

_____

_____

Is there anything we could have done better? _____

_____

_____

_____

_____

_____

About you...

Name (Mr/Mrs/Ms) _____

Address _____

_____ Zip _____

Daytime tel nos. _____

Which age group are you in?

Under 25 ☐   25–34 ☐   35–44 ☐   45–54 ☐   55–64 ☐   65+ ☐

How many trips do you make a year?

Less than one ☐   One ☐   Two ☐   Three or more ☐

Are you a AAA member?   Yes ☐   No ☐

Name of AAA club _____

About your trip

When did you book? m m / y y    When did you travel? m m / y y

How long did you stay? _____

Was it for business or leisure? _____

Did you buy any other travel guides for your trip?   Yes ☐   No ☐

If yes, which ones? _____

Thank you for taking the time to complete this questionnaire.